P9-CQM-263

# Inside the Soul of a new Generation

*Insights and Strategies for Reaching Busters*

# TIM CELEK & DIETER ZANDER

## WITH PATRICK KAMPERT

WILLOW CREEK RESOURCES

ZondervanPublishingHouse
*Grand Rapids, Michigan*

*A Division of* HarperCollins*Publishers*

**Authors' note**
Identities in this book have been changed to protect
the confidentiality of the persons involved.

---

*Inside the Soul of a New Generation*
Copyright © 1996 by Willow Creek Association

Requests for information should be addressed to:

📖 ZondervanPublishingHouse
*Grand Rapids, Michigan 49530*

**Library of Congress Cataloging-in-Publication Data**

Celak, Tim.
    Inside the soul of a new generation : insight and strategies for reaching
busters / Tim Celak and Dieter Zander, with Patrick Kampert.
        p.    cm.
    ISBN: 0-310-20594-8
    1. Church work with young adults. 2. Generation X—Psychology. 3.
Generation X—Religious life. 4. Intergenerational relations. 5. Evangelistic
work.  I. Zander, Dieter. II. Kampert, Patrick. III. Title.
BV4446.C45   1996
259'.2—dc 20                                   96-3870
                                                        CIP

*Edited by Mary McNeil*
*Cover design by Paula Gibson*
*Photography by LaBakk Studio*
*Interior design by Sherri L. Hoffman*

*Printed in the United States of America*

---

99  00  01  02 03 /❖ DH/ 10 9 8

*DZ—To Val: my wife, partner, lover, and friend.
And to Kyle, Conrad, and Christopher, who are convinced
that they, and everybody else in the world, are Baby Busters.
And to my two church families: New Song Church
and the Axis ministry at Willow Creek: Thanks for being
willing to follow the Lord and me in creating
new ministries for a new generation.*

*TC—To Sue, my partner in life and ministry and to my
daughters, Emily and Lauren, and to the people of Calvary
Church Newport Mesa, together we're making a difference.*

*PK—To my wife, Jan, a woman of beauty in every way.
And to our wonderful kids, April and Brent.*

91099

# Contents

# Foreword

Each generation presents the church with a fresh redemptive challenge—none more so than the twentysomething crowd. For the past twenty years at Willow Creek, we have attempted to make Christianity relevant to the generation of which the founding leaders are a part. In the past five years, we have become increasingly aware of the fact that the effectiveness of our approach to ministry has waned amongst Generation Xers. Feeling both frustrated and challenged, we began to try to understand the Busters and then to explore various ministry approaches that would capture their minds and hearts.

This book will benefit anyone whose heart beats fast for the next generation. Dieter Zander and Tim Celek have given their lives to the twenty-something crowd. They don't merely review sanitized statistics that most of us have already grown weary of reading, they write from the trenches of doing weekly ministry to Busters. They have not accommodated the Gospel to the next generation, but rather they have struggled to incarnate and explain the transforming power of Jesus Christ to Busters.

Jesus challenged his followers to observe the "signs of the times." We would do well to heed his warning, because the future is upon us, and the stakes of kingdom advancement have never been higher. May God stretch your vision and heart as he has mine through the courageous ministries of these two men.

BILL HYBELS
SENIOR PASTOR
WILLOW CREEK COMMUNITY CHURCH

# Acknowledgments

DZ—It's been twelve years since my wife and I started developing a church for a group we called the "people in-between" and who are now generally referred to as Baby Busters or Generation X. There are many who have shared this adventure with me and have contributed to what I've learned and experienced along the way. Thank you Val, Kyle, Conrad, and Christopher, my family, and Val's family for your love and support. I am grateful to the faculty of the International School of Theology for encouraging me to start a church while I was in seminary. And, in particular, to Ron Jenson and Don Weaver for their inspiration and instruction. Thanks to Rob Acker and the Community Baptist Church of Alta Loma for "mothering" but not smothering New Song Church. Thank you Bob and Janet Logan for the countless ways you have shared your wisdom and lives with us.

Thanks to all the New Song pioneers and those who eventually became our staff: Wes Wisham, Janine Letherer, Paul Kaak, Frank and Wendy Selvaggio, Scott Marshall, Kim Fundham, Eric and Senya Herron, Marilyn Faber, Duke Draeger, Dennis Bachman, Donna Spencer, Leslie Pope, Rochelle Cowper, and my assistant and friend, Susan Callow. Thanks also to those who served as our board of "youngers"—who eventually were old enough to be called elders—and to the many, many volunteers, in particular, Arnold Santos, who gave me back my weeknights by leading the bands. New Song Church, you helped demonstrate that it's possible to start and grow a church for Busters. Now you're living proof that Busters can lead churches and plant other Buster churches. Words cannot express how proud I am of you all.

I am also grateful to my new ministry team at Willow Creek Community Church. Together, we're trying to figure out how to help a Boomer church reach Busters, which is no simple challenge. Thanks to the Axis ministry core and staff, which is helping design this new ministry for a new generation: Rich and Deb Shurtz, Ted Beasley, Sandra Katz, and Lisa Kulpinski. I am grateful to Bill Hybels for his leadership and encouragement to reach the future of Willow Creek. Thanks also to John Burke for his support and to Jodi Walle, my assistant.

To Ann Spangler and Mary McNeil and the folks at Zondervan: Thanks for your patience with our first effort at putting these ideas on paper.

The adventure continues. Praise God!

TC—When I began my journey into church planting, I never fully realized how many people would cross my path and mark my life. It's been quite a ride over the years. I'm very grateful for the many people who have challenged and encouraged me along the way. First, a big thank you goes to my wife, Sue and my daughters, Emily and Lauren, you are the best. I will always appreciate Calvary Church of Santa Ana for launching me into pastoral ministry, as well as giving me the chance to plant a new church for a new generation. Thanks goes to Bill Hybels and Rick Warren for giving a "young" pastor the permission to venture out and try creative avenues in reaching the lost for Christ. I am deeply grateful for the personal mentoring and exchanges of wisdom by Bob Shank.

I am very thankful for the men and women of Calvary Church Newport Mesa. Together, we have ventured out on the edge extending the boundaries of God's Kingdom in new and exciting ways. In particular, Lane and Diane Kagey, Dale and Dawn Winson, Dave and Kathy Gentry, Ron and DeeAnn Gray, and John and Adele Duncan, your support of me and my family has been and continues to be huge, thanks. Thanks to the staff team of CCNM, many times I've felt like we are just kids playing church, yet God significantly uses us. Specifically, I am grateful for Dan Steward. You are a real model of godly authenticity. Ian and Terrilee Stevenson, Sue and I feel honored to have you and your family as close friends.

Thanks to Zondervan, Ann Spangler, and Mary McNeil for allowing "rookies" the chance to communicate our passion for reaching a new generation.

PK—Thanks to Dieter and Tim for the education, and to Ann Spangler for guidance and an intro into the book world. Thanks also to the people who generously shared ideas and experiences, including Ian Stevenson, Eric Briner, Barry Hovis, Victor Basquez, Kristine Wallace, Janet Logan, Frank and Wendy Selvaggio, Marlon Ramirez, Kim Fundum, George and Tara Masucci, Michelle Panlillio, Tom Garvey, Mark Hoelterhoff, Steve Mann, Paul Kaak, Jeremy Tucher, and Arne Carlson. And, last but far from least, to editor Mary McNeil for much patience.

# Introduction

Three scenes from the modern world:

## SCENE ONE, THE CHURCH

Greg is a pastor who has been successful at drawing the Baby Boom generation back to Christianity. But it nagged at him that young people weren't finding themselves comfortable in his church. He would deliver a compelling message that would move Boomers in his church, but the younger listeners seemed unimpressed. He thought perhaps reaching out to them one at a time might make a difference, so he had regularly been rearranging his schedule to get together with Matt, a young man in the so-called "Baby Buster" or "Generation X" age group.

Matt enjoyed their conversations and their outings as they began to get to know each other. He liked "hanging out," as he put it, with a pastor who didn't fit the stereotypes he'd believed about Christianity. But after several months, Greg, on the other hand, was starting to get frustrated.

"Nothing's happening," he said to a colleague. "Matt's no closer to showing an interest in Jesus than when we first started getting together. I'd like to give him a tract or something. But he shows no interest. It bothers me that I've invested all this time and nothing is being accomplished. There's no fruit from my efforts. I'm worried that I'm wasting my time—or worse, that I'm totally ineffective in relating to young people."

## SCENE TWO, THE OFFICE

Bill was fresh out of college and had landed a great entry-level job at one of the top firms in his field. Better yet, it was right in his hometown.

"He has a lot on the ball," admitted Sonja, his boss, "but I don't see much of a future for him. He's only out for himself. I tell you, these young people—every time they say something, it comes out sounding like a question. They sound unsure of themselves, like they're afraid to make a statement."

For his part, Bill can't understand what the fuss is about. "I'm a little leery of big companies; look at all the downsizing that's been going on. But I'm a hard worker; I just want everyone to get along. I don't like conflict, I never have. But so many jobs seem like they're designed to produce conflict, and I want no part of it."

## SCENE THREE, THE HOME

Grace was concerned when her daughter, Peggy, came home from college for the summer.

"I thought her nose was infected," she told her friend Joyce. "It looked like she had either had some acne trouble or that she had been cut by something. So I asked her about it and she said she had gotten her nose pierced at a rock festival. But the hole was starting to close up, and she actually had the nerve to ask me if I would pay for her to get it pierced again. I just don't understand it."

Have you ever encountered a situation similar to one of those described above? The truth is, many people are like Grace and her daughter—they just don't understand. And that's not too surprising. The world around us is changing at a rapidly accelerating pace. And as technology shifts that pace of life into overdrive, people are changing too.

Nowhere is this change more evident than in the lives of the Baby Buster generation. They've grown up quite differently than children of previous generations, and as a result, they think differently and act differently as well. Those of us who work with and among the Baby Busters see this reflected day in and day out. And, like Greg, Sonja, and Grace, we've had to work overtime to keep up with the changes these young adults are bringing to the world we know.

As pastors, we've had to create new paradigms for making Jesus relevant to a youth culture that has had very little positive exposure to Christianity. For more than a decade, it has been our joy—and, at times, our frustration—to work with Busters and encourage them to explore the radical impact that Jesus can have on their lives.

Dieter founded New Song Church in Covina, California, in 1984. At the time he left New Song in 1994 to create a ministry to Busters at Willow Creek Community Church in suburban Chicago, New Song's attendance was 1,200 people per weekend. The average age was twenty-six, and seventy percent were single. Tim founded Calvary Church Newport Mesa in Costa Mesa, California, in 1988. Today, 1,400 young people— many with no church background—arrive each weekend to hear the Gospel communicated in a fresh, culturally relevant manner.

When the two of us first crossed paths, it was only natural that we forge a close bond of friendship. Although churches geared toward Busters are beginning to sprout throughout the United States, there was a period of time when we were working this field alone. Those years of experience have, we hope, provided us with insights that may prove valuable to anyone trying to understand the next generation a little better—from pastors to Busters themselves.

Much has been written in Christian circles about the Baby Boom generation, and those books and articles have been quite valuable in translating the Gospel into a language that that age group can comprehend. But very little has been written about the unique challenge posed by the next generation—and as Busters have begun to reach the age of thirty, it behooves us to begin to address their spiritual search before the pace of the culture moves them beyond our reach.

Why should Busters matter to us? Because they matter to God. Busters are the lost coin that Jesus alluded to in Luke 15. They are the prodigal sons and daughters weaned on a diet of hopeless nihilism that has left them peculiarly empty and hungry.

We hope that our words and our experience will encourage you to accept Busters, value Busters, and try to understand Busters. Whatever you find useful in these pages, cling to. Bear in mind that, by necessity, we are dealing to some extent with generalizations. All human beings are different, "fearfully and wonderfully made" creations of God. But many Busters share some similar qualities. We hope we've sketched some ways for you to begin to look at the next generation through God's eyes, through the eyes of the waiting Father who beckons his long-lost children home.

# Part 1

## Generation Angst

# Chapter 1

# Who Are the Busters?

Since my youth, O God, you have taught me, and to this day I declare your marvelous deeds. Even when I am old and gray, do not forsake me, O God, till I declare your power to the next generation, your might to all who are to come.

—Psalm 71:17–18

Margaret watched scornfully as Jenny and Jeff laughed, hooted, and hollered as they careened like bearings in a tilted pinball machine across the grounds of the youth summer camp.

Normally, Margaret wouldn't have flicked an eyebrow at such activity at the camp—kids are supposed to have fun, after all—but this brother and sister weren't kids, they were young adults. "Why don't they grow up and act their age?" Margaret thought to herself.

Jenny and Jeff were friends of Margaret and her family. They had grown up in an evangelical home that, like about half the marriages in this country, imploded in divorce. To some extent, Jenny and Jeff had been reeling ever since. Margaret and her husband regularly opened up their home to young people with various hurts and needs, and the guests (usually in their late teens and early twenties) were always quite curious—

and a bit amazed—at what a stable home looked like and how it functioned. Jenny and Jeff were two such onlookers.

Margaret accompanied them on their impromptu "road trip," a visit to the camp they had enjoyed as children. The nostalgic surroundings unveiled a side of them that Margaret hadn't seen before. It was cute at first, but then she started to get annoyed. She was about to say something, but then stopped short when the realization splashed her like a camper's water balloon: "They're acting like this because they're going back to a time and place where they felt safe. A time when their world was whole. A time they haven't known since."

Margaret shared that story with us at one of the seminars we've conducted on the so-called "Baby Busters" (also labeled "Generation X" by many in the media), and it captures quite clearly some of the problems that the next generation has been quietly grappling with as it comes of age. And that age has been a long time coming.

## DEMOGRAPHICS

Who are the Busters? As we shall see, this group really is more of an attitude than a definitive demographic bracket. And surprisingly, this attitude seems to be shared, in most respects, by both male and female Busters. Buster traits appear to transcend gender. Here's how the generational breakdown looks: Seniors (born before 1925), Builders (1925–1944), Baby Boomers (1945–1964), Baby Busters (1965–1980), and Blasters (born after 1980). Thus, for our purposes, the Baby Buster generation consists of the 46 million people born in the U.S. between 1965 and 1980.

Forty-six million is not a small group. In fact, the Busters are the second-largest generation in history after the 72-million-strong Boomers. However, due to the sharp decline in birth rates, which began around 1963, they were named Baby Busters.

We use the term *Buster* because it not only describes the post-Boomer demographic reality, but also because it describes the attitude of this particular generation. When you think of a "boom," you think in terms of something that's expanding and moving forward like a "boom town" filled with potential. That's how many Baby Boomers have always considered their world. But a lot of the Busters see their world as busted, as broken.

The Buster generation is the first in many generations that is not inheriting a lifestyle superior to that of their parents, and the Busters harbor a lot of resentment because of that. In many Busters' eyes, the economy has been trashed, leaving an enormous national debt that the Busters will get the bill for. Unemployment among Busters is dangerously near Depression-era levels. The sexual revolution spawned in the '60s is shot through with the ravages of AIDS. The "tune in, turn on, drop out" drug experiment has twisted into a spiraling cyclone of crack and violence. The "disposable society" has bequeathed environmental chaos, a land of landfills, and toxic Superfund cleanups. No wonder that *U.S. News and World Report* dubbed Busters "The Fix-It Generation." There's a lot that needs fixing. There's a lot that's busted.

Busters, say Neil Howe and Bill Strauss in their seminal book, *13th Gen*, have experienced "the betrayed expectations of a youth world that went from sweet to sour as they approached it." How sour can it be for some kids in the next generation? Howe and Strauss outline a pretty bleak house in one paragraph:

> Every day, over 2,500 American children witness the divorce or separation of their parents. Every day, 90 kids ... are committed to foster homes. Every day, thirteen Americans age 15 to 24 commit suicide, and another sixteen are murdered. Every day, the typical 14-year-old watches 3 hours of TV and does 1 hour of homework. Every day, over 2,200 kids drop out of school. Every day, 3,610 teenagers are assaulted, 630 are robbed, and 80 are raped.... Every day, 1,000 unwed teenage girls become mothers.[1]

Those are not ideal conditions for developing the life skills and maturity needed for succeeding in relationships and the workplace. One would think that their elders, cognizant of the difficulties the Busters have faced, would be sympathetic and helpful, but that's often not the case. Increasingly, in the media and in social situations, the Busters are the targets of jokes, complaints, and slanderous comments.

How are Busters responding to the busted condition of the world they are inheriting and how do they feel about prevailing attitudes toward their generation? Sometimes they respond with anger. Other times with apathy—a shrug of the shoulders and a quiet "whatever." But we've noticed an increasing amount of creative thought and energy being directed toward developing new ways of relating, new ways of creating, and new ways of addressing the brokenness that surrounds them. So, although we refer to them as Busters, the future holds the hope that in time, much of their world will be less "busted" than it is now.

## THE PROBLEM WITH LABELS

Busters don't like labels. They see a name like "Buster" or "Twentysomething" or "Generation X" as a stamp imposed from without by older members of the media and society. A label signifies that someone is putting them in a box so they can be controlled and manipulated, and many Busters hate that. As Douglas Coupland wrote in *Generation X*, the novel that gave birth to the movement, "I am not a target market." A label gives rise to an us-versus-them mentality in the mind of a Buster: "If you say I'm a Buster, then I'm segregated in that group. Why can't I just be a person? Why can't you just be a person? And why can't we relate together as people?"

Adam Silverman, a successful young entrepreneur, told *Forbes* magazine that "the whole Generation X/Slacker thing is a complete media fabrication."

It's true that the Busters are a diverse lot. But they're beginning to gain a sense of identity. In a recent MTV poll, a majority (58 percent) of the sixteen- to twenty-nine-year-olds surveyed nationally say they see themselves as "a distinct generation." What they would call themselves lacks a consensus, perhaps a reflection of their disdain for labels. Thirty-one percent opted for "Twentysomethings"—which becomes erroneous when you realize that the oldest Busters have now hit the thirty mark. In the poll, preference for the Generation X moniker was close behind at thirty percent.

The population figures for the Busters can be a bit fuzzy depending on where you mark the parameters of the age group. (In fact Douglas Coupland himself, the literary guru of Generation X, was born in 1961.) But as we stated before, being a Buster has more to do with attitude than with age. We know many people in their mid twenties who are organized, driven, career-minded people who seem more like Boomers than Busters. And yet we know many people in their thirties who are more attuned to the attitude and mindset of Busters.

But when people try to define and label Busters, they often have a "slacker" image in mind: disheveled clothes, multiple piercings of ears and other body parts, goatees on men, and a cynical attitude. Yet we know Busters in all shapes and sizes: yes, slackers, but also young conservatives, black-leather-clad rebels, retro-minded neo-hippies and, mostly, average-looking young men and women who share some common life experiences.

They're a diverse bunch—in more ways than one.

## DIVERSITY 101

When Dieter left New Song Church in Southern California in 1994 to develop a ministry for Busters at Willow Creek Community Church in suburban Chicago, one of the things he missed most was the cultural diversity. New Song had people from all ethnic backgrounds and Southern California life was a festival of color and culture. The suburbs of Chicago are predominantly white middle class. That's slowly changing, and one of the issues in developing a church service specifically for

Busters at Willow Creek is encouraging diversity. In fact, for one young woman who is among the core of Buster leaders at Willow Creek, integrating the church and presenting it as a model for racial unity and cooperation has been the driving force for her involvement in the Buster ministry.

The Buster generation isn't a White Anglo-Saxon Protestant phenomenon. As we'll explore in part 2, the forces that have shaped the Busters' identity have played a role in the lives of all who have been born or raised in America—and, in many instances, the world—over the last three decades.

Busters are the most racially diverse generation in U.S. history. Whites now comprise less than seventy-five percent of the Buster population in America, and immigration and birth rates will make that number shrink over the years, as will the fact that the white population has an older median age than other ethnic groups in the U.S.; Hispanics are the youngest with a median age of twenty-six.

All this diversity doesn't mean that all Busters adhere religiously to the politically correct movement. "Some Xers," writes advertising executive Karen Ritchie in *Marketing to Generation X*, "particularly those in large multicultural cities like New York, simply wrap themselves in indifference, believing it the best way to avoid confrontation."[2]

Another factor, of course, is that Busters, who grew up feeling unwanted and alienated, don't want anyone else to have to experience the frustration of being the outsider. They find irony in the PC movement (witness the success of James Finn Garner's best-selling satirical *Politically Correct Bedtime Stories*) but worry whether it will so fragment the country that the melting pot that used to be America will boil over and explode into a new tribalism. In general, say Howe and Strauss, the Busters are increasingly aware that any change must begin with them: "The accumulated failures of elder-built racial policies have led to . . . a profound skepticism about any social unit larger than the individual or family."[3]

## GENERATION ANGST

Kurt Cobain of the rock band Nirvana was the John Lennon of his generation until he committed suicide with a shotgun blast to the head in 1994. Cobain was a reluctant spokesman. He said he wasn't trying to speak for anyone but himself in the rage and alienation of his lyrics and said he realized that his problems were probably minor compared to others'. "I'm a product of a spoiled America.... There are so many worse things than a divorce. I've just been brooding and bellyaching about something I couldn't have, which is a family, a solid family unit."

Ultimately, Cobain couldn't cope with the pain. Many around us are still enmeshed in the battle. "The dissolution of the American family has exerted a tremendous torque on the members of Cobain's generation," noted Sarah Ferguson in the *Utne Reader,* the insightful *Reader's Digest* of the alternative press.

Besides the anger that many Busters feel over their busted world (indeed, 45 percent of the Busters in the MTV poll described themselves as angry), their angst often expresses itself in three other ways.

*They feel alone.* Feeling alone is different from feeling lonely. Loneliness is the experience of having no one around with whom to connect. Aloneness is the experience of being in a crowd and being unable to connect with people in a deeply fulfilling manner.

*They feel abandoned.* Anyone who has spent any length of time with young people realizes that they struggle with abandonment issues. As a result, it's often difficult to get close to Busters. They hold you off at arm's length because they're worried about being abandoned and hurt in the same way that their families abandoned and hurt them.

*They feel alienated.* They have a deep need for reconciliation with other people because of the conflict they have experienced in their lives. Alienation is the feeling of estrangement that many Busters experience. When your family situation is less than ideal, you don't learn the skills needed to form the deep friendships that everyone needs for emotional health. You're always on the outside looking in, and this is reflected in the Buster culture. Look, for example, at MTV's controversial *Beavis and Butthead* show. If you get beyond some of the scripts' crudity, you find a couple of nerdy guys who are always laughing at other people—but they never seem to truly connect with anyone, including each other. "Deep down," pollster Barna writes, "a majority of Busters struggle with feelings of alienation. They feel estranged from family, from community, from God, and often from self."

Many Busters have gotten to the point where they feel they can trust only themselves. They feel like they have been cheated by the government, by the economy, by their families, and by previous generations in many ways. They don't have a lot of faith in institutions—political, religious, or financial. They see the world through a cloud of cynicism and skepticism.

Taken to its extreme, alienation is one of the root causes in the rate of suicide, which is up 300 percent from the previous generation. "Most experts attribute youth suicide to *anomie*," writes sociologist and journalist Donna Gaines in her compelling book *Teenage Wasteland*. "In an anomic suicide, the individual isn't connected to the society.... To be anomic is to feel disengaged, adrift, alienated. Like you don't fit in anywhere."[4]

## DISPELLING THE SLACKER MYTH

Besides jokes about angst, Busters commonly must learn to deal with a frustrating foe: the stereotype of the slacker. In our decade of dealing with Busters, we've found this to be utter nonsense. In 1994, *Newsweek* devoted a cover story to debunking myths about the Busters. Jeff Giles' "Generalizations X" placed the slacker story as Myth Number One, noting that "most of the bad PR comes from Boomers, who seem engaged in what Coupland called 'clique maintenance.'"

But the tide may be beginning to turn. The business world is at the forefront of seeing how young people are making a difference. *Forbes* magazine says Busters are just what American business needs: "Grungy? Maybe. Lazy and apathetic? Not at all. The so-called Generation X is the most entrepreneurial generation in American history.... This is America's first Computer Generation, and it is beginning to combine technology and human freedom in ways that promise to restore this country to economic leadership."

The myth has its roots in the misunderstanding that exists between the Boomers and Busters, which we'll detail in the next chapter. We're not saying that Busters are right and Boomers are wrong when they interact with each other, we're merely saying that what they have in common is an ample amount of misunderstanding and miscommunication. "They just don't get it," say the Busters. "They just don't get it," say the Boomers. Actually, neither side gets it. In "Don't Call Me Slacker," *Fortune* magazine's profile of the Top 20 Twentysomethings in business, consultant Maury Hanigan noted: "These young managers come with skills that companies wish they could instill in older workers—computer literacy, an understanding of diversity, a global mindset. But companies don't know how to manage the Xers."

The misunderstandings that often exist between the Busters and previous generations can only be dispelled through a concerted effort toward the development of relationships. In the context of relationship, new understanding takes place, acceptance flourishes, and personal value is communicated from one generation to another.

In the pages to come, we hope to help you understand the traits characteristic of many Busters and how such knowledge can help you more effectively reach out to them in friendship and community.

# Chapter 2

# Of Boomers and Busters

Like quiet younger brothers and sisters, we lie in wait,
looking for ways to be different from our older siblings.

—Steven Gibb

Before Tim started Calvary Church Newport Mesa in Costa
Mesa, California, he was the singles pastor at a megachurch
in Southern California. One of his responsibilities was to over-
see a board comprised of church members. Most of the people
on the board were older Boomers, but there was one young
man named Brad who was twenty years old. Brad had a tendency to miss meetings from time to time because of business
commitments, which was understandable. As a successful busi-
nessman and a church board member, it was obvious Brad had
a lot going for him.

Dave was another board member who wasn't always
around. Again, it wasn't a problem. Dave was in his early fifties
and worked in a different industry than Brad, but he had similar obligations that kept him away from the board from time to
time. But the other board members didn't see the parallel. If
Dave was absent and someone asked where he was, the
response would be, "Oh, he's on an important business trip."
But if Brad didn't show up, or was even late, the grumbling
would start. "This guy's never here. And when he is, he's never
on time. He's just a flake."

When Boomers and Busters interact, the result often tends to be like combining oil and water. That's because they have different agendas, different values, and different ways of operating as they pursue those varying goals. It doesn't make one generation valuable and one worthless, or one generation right and the other wrong, it merely means that they're on different wavelengths. Everyone is engaged in the pursuit of happiness; it's just a question of how you go about it.

The Boomers have basked in the spotlight all their lives, by dint of their sheer numbers alone. As children, they were the center of their parents' lives and, by extension, American society. They may not have always had a *Father Knows Best* or *Ozzie and Harriet* existence, but there can be no denying that the Boomers had a sense of safety and security in their formative years that the Busters never knew. When the tumult of the '60s arrived, Boomers thrived, donning their countercultural cloaks and capturing the attention of the world. Civil-rights laws changed, universities altered their curriculums as they bowed to student protests, Woodstock became an event and then an icon for the twentieth century, and the war in Vietnam came to a close partly as a result of Boomer protests. Yet when it was time to move on, many Boomers cut their hair, put the peace signs in storage, and grew wealthy the Wall Street way in the '80s.

"At their core," says Karen Ritchie, who considers herself a Boomer at fifty-two, "Boomers are idealists, who sincerely believe that the ideas they subscribe to are more important than the comfort or welfare of other people."

## THE NEW GENERATION GAP

Busters are not idealists, they're pragmatists. They have to be. The only great expectations they have are of massive taxes to pay off the deficit.

"No one was ever supposed to be younger than we are," said the New Republic's Michael Kinsley, with tongue (and truth) embedded in Boomer cheek.

"Boomers have developed a peculiar blindness to Generation X," adds Ritchie. "This oversight has arisen partly from a natural desire to think of themselves as young, and from an instinct to preserve their own hard-won base of power."[1]

What Boomers fail to realize is that Busters have never wanted to rule the world. They merely want to rule their own individual destinies.

## CONQUEST VS. COMMUNITY

Doing business in Argentina is different than doing business in the United States. For instance, take a look at the differences between a sixty-minute business meeting with Americans in the U.S. and the same meeting with Argentinians in Argentina.

In the U.S., when you're greeting someone, he or she might say to you, "Hi! How are you doing? How's your family?" You respond, "Fine, just fine," and go on from there and transact your business. It's understood that you're not to get immersed in a deep discussion at that point; it's an exchange of pleasantries prior to fifty minutes of business.

In Argentina, it's just the opposite. You take fifty minutes to talk about your family and your relationships, and then you consummate the business part in the last ten minutes. Are the Argentinians wrong for not doing things our way? No, they merely have different values. It's the same way with the Busters.

For better or worse, the Boomers have accomplished a lot during their time on Planet Earth. They're a cause-oriented, mission-minded bunch. They like nothing better than diving into a major project. When Bill Clinton, a Boomer, became president, what was one of the first tasks he tried to tackle? The reformation of the health-care system. Is there a bigger job than that for those in government? Boomers are a generation that seeks to *conquer*.

Busters, on the other hand, don't want to conquer. They want to connect with other people; they want to experience *community*. In their eyes, conquering is an us-versus-them proposition, and one side will be vanquished. For Busters, the question isn't "How can I get ahead?" The question is "How can we get along?"

Mario's story illustrates this point. At twenty-five, Mario's combination of skill, experience, and youth made him an ideal candidate for advancement in the burgeoning software industry.

When opportunity knocked in the form of a better job with more money, Mario turned it down. He'd have to move fifty miles away, and he didn't want to leave the relationships he had formed in his small group at New Song. Busters will often choose relationships over raises, and maintaining their community over climbing the corporate ladder. They clearly value community over conquest.

Both on the job and off, relationships are important to Busters. Though they may take a lot longer to develop, we know from experience that such relationships are well worth the trouble. Think back, for a moment, to Jesus and his disciples. They spent time together eating leisurely meals, sitting and talking, walking from town to town. And though time may be more difficult to spare today than two thousand years ago, Busters usually find a way to spend it with their friends.

"The power of friendships among Busters should not be underestimated," writes Barna. "When they engage in their favorite leisure activity, the majority of these young adults (53 percent) do so with their friends."

Clearly, at home and at work, Busters value community over conquest.

## PRODUCT VS. PROCESS

A close cousin of the conquest vs. community dichotomy that exists between Boomers and Busters is product vs. process. Many Boomers have a "cut to the chase" mentality; results are what matter most. Busters most often have a "kick back and chill" mentality, again valuing relationships over results.

Dale, the pastor of a Buster church, was interviewing Tom, a twenty-five-year-old applicant for the post of music director. Dale was trying to ask Tom about his background, about what kind of experience he'd had musically. Yet even with Dale's years of working with Busters, he was starting to get a little frustrated. He was trying to get to the point, and Tom's point was all about just hanging out and getting to know each other.

"So, tell me some more about your family," Tom said. "How old are your kids?"

"I was thinking to myself, 'Who's interviewing whom here?'" Dale remembers. "I wanted to get through the interview, and Tom just wanted to shoot the breeze."

For many Boomers, the end result is what matters. But most Busters simply have a different value. The process by which you accomplish something, not just the product, is what counts. A Buster will often ask himself or herself questions like: Was it fair? Was it just? Did it make sense? Did I feel valued? Was I empowered? These are process-oriented questions. Tom was more involved with the process than the end product.

## LIVE TO WORK VS. WORK TO LIVE

The title of this section may be on the verge of becoming a cliché in the area of generational studies, but that's only because of its ring of truth when it comes to Boomers and Busters.

Boomers tend to see work as a fulfilling end in itself. Busters see work as a means to an end. Liz Landon is one of the Busters that *Fortune* magazine profiled as one of the top twentysomethings in business, but it's apparent her values are in a different place than her generational predecessors. She says her hero is George Bailey, Jimmy Stewart's lovable character in *It's A Wonderful Life*, Frank Capra's classic film. Bailey, notes Landon, "wasn't terribly successful in business, but he was successful in life."

The financial boom of the '80s fueled the Boomers' lifestyle of luxury. Although many Boomers are reevaluating what it cost them, some have grown accustomed to such a standard—and they're not likely to make any detours on their career pathways. They do indeed live to work.

Busters have never had such an option. Aside from exceptions like Landon, their job prospects remain limited regardless of how much schooling they have. They've also learned from the mistakes of their parents—they're more inclined to put family first. Busters work to live. Ritchie says that young women today "put a greater importance on the home and family life they missed as children and are unwilling to compromise that ideal for a job."

That attitude flabbergasts Boomers, especially Boomer women who struggled mightily to achieve some measure of equal footing in the workplace and now see that the younger generation is unimpressed with the trail they blazed. Work merely provides Busters with the money necessary to survive. They find fulfillment in friends and family, not career.

But some Busters lean too heavily on this attitude as an excuse for being less than productive workers.

"Imagine that you are designing a T-shirt for today's younger worker," poses a question put forth by Lawrence J. Bradford and Claire Raines in their book *Twentysomething*. "What slogan would you emblazon on the front? The question 'When do I get an office?' might not be too far off the mark."[2]

"[Busters] are not motivated by work," concludes pollster Barna. "It is a necessary but unappealing means to an end."

## INDIVIDUAL VS. TEAM

Read any of the latest books on management? One concept seems to come back again and again: the team approach.

Busters may not have introduced the team model, but it is not so surprising that the idea is flowering as the next generation comes of age.

The team approach is a very different scenario from the Boomers' heyday in the 1980s when the individual was stressed and, indeed, championed. Donald Trump. Ivan Boesky. Steven Jobs. Lee Iacocca. Michael Milken. The Boomers are mavericks in their mentality, autonomous in their attitude.

Call it "Do Your Own Thing" vs. "Do Our Own Thing." Call it "The Me Generation" vs. "The We Generation." Call it what you will, but Busters are more interested in doing things as a team.

They would rather do things together than have any one of their own peer group elevated above the others to the top. Even their culture reflects this: Their first coming-of-age movie was *The Breakfast Club.* They date in groups. They dance in groups. They shop in groups. The era of the individual has ended. A new era of team and community has arrived. Even on television, the hit show, *Friends,* is all about a group, a community, a team. The actors and actresses in the cast are quite close off the set as well (they're known for gathering at one of their homes to watch the show each week), and that genuineness comes through to the Busters around the country.

## ACTIVE VS. REACTIVE

When Boomers act, Busters react. Whatever the action, Busters tend to do the exact opposite. They've lived in the shadow of the Boomers for so long that, in their frustration, they're determined to find a way to forge their own identity, which often looks like the flip side of the Boomer. It's like a youth growing up in the shadow of a starlike older brother or sister. He or she generally chooses to emulate the older sibling or selects the black-sheep option of rebellion. The latter choice can be unfortunate, because there is much in the Boomer generation worth imitating—focus, direction, idealism, work ethic, perseverance.

Boomers who are trying to reach out to the next generation would do well to keep the reactive nature of this generation in mind as they interact with young people. Because, underneath the sheen of cynicism and skepticism, most Busters dearly want to establish relationships with the older people around them. They just don't know how to go about it. And they're not sure if it's even possible.

Many Busters come from flawed families and are groping around for support, validation, and nurturing. They need to be able to find that in the church, because those are scarce commodities in society at large. You may not agree with everything they say or do, but don't let that hinder your hand of help. Just be real. Be honest. Try to understand them, accept them, and value them. You'll be surprised at how warmly Busters will respond toward you.

At a seminar we conducted on ministering to Busters a couple years ago, a Boomer pastor said to us jokingly, "They're not going to go away, are they?" No, they're not. And they're probably not going to change either, which is a topic we'll explore in the next chapter.

# Chapter 3

# My So-called Life: Will the Busters Grow Up?

I won't grow up.

—Peter Pan

Don is a Buster in his early twenties who sometimes frustrates older family members and friends. He switched majors halfway through college, moving from the education field to a marketing emphasis. He took longer to complete his degree than some other young adults from his town—five and a half years instead of the standard four. Now he works in a department store. Though the Sunday paper is full of help-wanted ads in marketing, Don hasn't applied for any of them.

"I'm not sure what I want to do," he says.

But he knows whatever he ends up in, it probably won't be marketing. He's decided he doesn't really like marketing. He felt pressured by his family to "pick something—anything" as a new major.

"It was the thing to do at the time," he says.

Now he's unsure of himself, and the older Boomers in his family circle are, you might say, circling the wagons, preparing for battle over his indecision. What compounds their exasperation is Linda, Don's wife. Linda is very Boomer-oriented in her decision-making process; she's wanted to be a nurse since she was a child, got her degree in four years, and is now going back for extra schooling. That's the way to do it, Don's family voices approvingly.

Don, meanwhile, could very easily take management training classes for his job, but he isn't sure he wants to make retail a career either. "That's part of the problem," he admits.

Don may be an atypical Buster in the sense that he married right after college, but many in his age group can relate to his indecision over a career choice. It's a major commitment, and not one to be taken lightly. Besides, in today's business world, a career doesn't mean forever anymore. One study cited by Barna says Busters can be expected to change careers—not just jobs—at least six times during their adult years. With downsizing and mergers a frequent occurrence in the marketplace, Busters may be correct in their skepticism over corporate stability.

## THE "POSTPONED GENERATION"

Are Busters immature? Are they childish? Will they ever change and take on more of the characteristics of the people we generally call "adults"?

That depends on your definition and your perspective. Where do you obtain your information about Busters' behavior and values? Well, some of it comes from personal observation, usually by people older than the Busters. Other information is gleaned from the observations of the media outlets, which are managed, in most cases, by Boomers and Builders.

So what you have is a perspective on young people filtered through a different standard. The world has changed—and continues to change—profoundly since the '60s, which is when the leading edge of the Boomers came of age and when the lens through which they view the world was formed. It could be argued that Busters are being held to a standard that does not apply to them, that is forged from a time and place largely alien to them.

Some of this may merely be wistfulness. Some Boomers spent their early adult years climbing the corporate ladder and are now growing reflective about some of the experiences they sacrificed along the way.

Groused one prep school senior quoted in *13th Gen:* "There's nothing so pathetic as someone at 40 trying to act like they're 22 because when they were 22 they acted like they were 40."

Sometimes, Boomers and Busters act even younger than that. Blockbuster, the corporate behemoth built on Wayne Huizenga's video-store empire, is launching a chain of adult indoor playgrounds called Block Party, similar to the Discovery Zone chain that caters to small children. Now, adults can jump in the plastic ball pit and crawl through tunnels too.

If Boomers are reconnecting with their childhood, many Busters never really had one. "Because of the divorce rate, I think we had to grow up too fast," one Buster told us.

This may be one reason why Busters are hesitant to cross over once they arrive at the threshold of adulthood. "Prior generations," writes Barna in *Baby Busters,* "couldn't wait to reach the 'age of reason' so that they could launch out on their own." That is not the case with the Busters. They see no "standard" for adulthood, they're insecure about themselves and their ability to maintain relationships, they've been conditioned to trust nothing but their own experience, and they're uncertain about the future. It's no wonder they're hesitant to take on the trappings that society has come to expect from the post twenty-one crowd.

Thus, in a sense, Busters are indeed the "Postponed Generation," as Susan Littwin's landmark book of ten years ago described them:

- Like Don, they're waiting longer and longer to decide on a career, and satisfaction—not money—is the primary driving force.

- Today, nearly six out of ten people between the ages of twenty and twenty-four are living with their parents. Seen through a wider age span, about thirty percent of the eighteen to thirty-four age group are living at home. While this is primarily an economic consideration, it's also true that some members of the young "fix-it" generation are strengthening relationships with their parents in their adulthood, something they missed while growing up.
- Marketing expert Karen Ritchie notes that women in the Buster demographic are "under less financial pressure to find a husband early."
- Given the rocky relationships they witnessed growing up, Buster men and women are delaying marriage. The average age at which adults marry is now about twenty-five and rising. About thirty percent of men and twenty percent of women between the ages of thirty and thirty-four have never married.

Postponed? Yes. Will they grow up? Maybe they are grown-up, and maybe it just doesn't fit the mold of the previous generations.

## A DIFFERENT LOOK

At New Song Church, the average age of the people who attend is twenty-six, and seventy percent of them are single. At Calvary, most are in their late twenties and the majority also are unmarried. Many still live at home. But most will marry, have children, raise children. Those who can afford it will buy homes.

The hard part is that there have been few decent role models for this generation. Thus, with each different life skill, mentoring will be invaluable to Busters. But each stage of the Busters' lives will look different than the Boomers' experiences.

Many things in life are cyclical. Nations move from conservative governments to liberal ones and back again. Economies fluctuate between prosperity and recession. Howe and Strauss quite convincingly make a case in comparing Busters to the "Lost Generation" of Ernest Hemingway and Gertrude Stein.

But even as they move into more familiar patterns of adulthood, this generation is not going to grow up to become Boomers. A forty-year-old Buster will not be like a forty-year-old Boomer because of lifelong exposure to the four major societal forces—postmodernity, the broken and blended family, the media, and the economy—that have shaped their lives. As we will see, these forces are unlikely to disappear anytime soon. Future generations (the Boomlets and beyond) are more likely to resemble the Buster generation because they're growing up in a similar environment. Thus, it would be foolish to assume that Busters are an aberrational blip on the generational screen; if anything, the qualities that Busters possess may intensify in future generations, for better or worse.

Exactly how all this will play out remains to be seen. But there will be a great hunger for belonging. We think there will be an all-out quest among Busters to make families work, and a search for truth and spiritual fulfillment. But before we can invite them into communities of belonging, help them with their families, and guide them in their search for truth and spiritual fulfillment, we must first understand what makes Busters tick, which is a topic we'll explore in part 2.

# Part 2

## Bend Me, Shape Me
## (Major Shaping Forces)

# Chapter 4

# Anything Goes

The end of the moral interpretation of the world ...
leads to nihilism.

—Friedrich Nietzsche

Gretchen is involved in youth ministry and was chatting with a Buster named Andy about Christianity. Eventually, the discussion turned to some serious philosophical issues that Andy was having problems with. They started talking about the concept of sin and how it separates us from God, and how much God wants to forgive us our sins and restore us to the intimate relationship with him that he originally intended.

"There is nothing you've done in your life that God can't forgive," Gretchen told him. As an example, she mentioned the case of Jeffrey Dahmer, the Milwaukee man who murdered and cannibalized his young male victims. Dahmer himself was later murdered in prison.

"God is even willing to forgive a person like Jeffrey Dahmer if he repents," Gretchen said. "His grace is big enough that it can cover the sins of Jeffrey Dahmer."

"So what's wrong with Jeffrey Dahmer?" Andy asked.

Gretchen wasn't sure how to take that response. Maybe he was joking. "Well," she said, "he killed people. And then he ate them."

"So what?" Andy said. "We eat animals."

Andy wasn't kidding. How do you answer that line of thinking? It wasn't just a matter of Andy having different values, it was as if he had no values at all, no boundaries. Admittedly, this is an extreme, though true, example. But it illustrates the logical drift of a worldview that has no moorings.

Nietzsche's "end of the moral interpretation of the world" is here. We live in an age of postmodernity, and if that sounds like a difficult concept to grasp, bear with us. If you had to break it down to two words, try these: Anything goes.

The Busters were the first generation to grow up in the postmodern era, and it's had a tremendous impact on them. They were the first generation to work their way through a completely secular public school system, where they learned that truth was an entirely subjective matter: There are no absolutes; everything's relative.

Therefore, a postmodern person's attitude might be, "Let's respect each other's truths. You have your truth; I have my truth. That's fine for you. Your truth may be radically different from my truth, but since this generation values a sense of community above all else, diametrically opposed truths can coexist. It may be a paradox, but that's okay." Thus, Andy's viewpoint is of equal value with any other perspective.

Postmodernism is the school of thought that says all truth is subjective. It's the flip side of modernism, which has been the philosophical principle undergirding the Western world since the Enlightenment. Modernism shook up many in the religious community because it dethroned God and made human beings the center of the universe.

The Enlightenment, knowledge, reason, and logic were seen as the keys to power. Natural laws were in operation that controlled the universe; all humans had to do was scientifically discover and apply those laws. From John Locke to Isaac Newton, the Enlightenment changed the way we looked at the world. "Although modernism did not emerge all at once," says psychologist David Elkind in *Ties That Stress*, "it did have a central, unifying theme: celebration of the individual over established authority."

Modernists believed that empiricism could help us to understand truth; in other words, "We can scientifically figure things out and we can technologically make things better." Progress makes perfect.

In modernism, since truth had to be proven, everyone was on the same page. "In a word, the epitome of modernism was unity: unity of truth, unity of self, unity of words and meaning, a unified state, a view of history as unitary and moving in one direction, relative conformity in the way of life and the views of those who count," writes USC professor Robert S. Ellwood in *The Sixties, Spiritual Awakening*.[1]

Modernism started fraying at the edges around the time Nietzsche declared that God was dead. Einstein's theory of relativity hastened the rise of postmodernism, but the movement really started taking hold on college campuses in the late 1960s. To put it very simply, scholars started seeing that, for every question science answered, new gaps in knowledge arose. And the idea that science and technology could solve all our problems and make a better world went the way of the Ford Model T, itself a product of the Industrial Revolution, which ultimately cheapened human life as the advent of mass production glorified "progress."

On the campus, notes Ellwood, the idea that modernism produced "conformity" was a death knell. Who decided whose views were more important than others? "The problem was that to those elite who best embody and perpetuate modernism's leading values, all other people are marginalized to varying degrees," he writes.[2] Can you see how this led to the politically correct movement?

In spiritual terms, the "everything is relative" school of theology did away with the idea that there are any absolute truths in the world. Everything is subject to your own interpretation.

Thus, as Canadian philosophy professor George Englebretsen put it in a witty put-down of postmodernism, "There is no truth. Or, to be fair, there is no Truth. There are lots of little truths, all of which are relative to the social, psychological, historical, political, etc., contexts of their utterances."

With the foundation of any basis of right and wrong now demolished, society started to move away from the idea that something could be proved logically. In earlier days, you could use logic to help people understand the validity of Christianity. C. S. Lewis was a master of logic in showing a war-torn England why Jesus' claims to be the Messiah made logical sense. Logic has also been a staunch, longtime ally of Josh McDowell, who has inspired countless people with his historical evidences for the veracity of the Bible and Jesus' life, and thus the myriad Messianic prophecies of the Old Testament that Jesus fulfilled. But in the postmodern age, logic and historical facts alone won't cut it.

## ONLY EXPERIENCES NEED APPLY

A postmodern mind, presented with seemingly irrefutable logic and a pile of verifiable facts, is likely to say, "So what? That's your bag. If it works for you, great. But don't force it on me."

The postmodern Busters have no faith in institutions. They trust only themselves. They don't approach truth and say, "I can prove it." They will trust only their own experience to decide if something is worthy of their attention or not. Barna's research backs this up: "To the typical Buster, there is no such thing as absolute truth. Statistically, 70% claim that absolute truth does not exist, that all truth is relative and personal."

It's hard to blame them for their skepticism. In government, the legacy of Watergate lingers to this day. Many of their families failed them. As far as Christianity is concerned, their chief frame of reference is the fall of prominent TV evangelists.

Science and technology? They may love their computers, but the defining moment for many of them was when the Challenger space shuttle blew up and killed some of the best and brightest America had to offer. Science and technology produced enough nuclear weapons, Agent Orange, and napalm to give nightmares to the Busters' parents; and some of the Busters who served in the Persian Gulf War returned home with a host of mysterious ailments that they attribute to everything from Iraqi chemical weapons to the burning oil fields of Kuwait. Science and technology solve nothing, say Busters. So, with no truth to hang onto and no hope of bettering humanity through science and technology, Busters find themselves in a type of moral, philosophical, spiritual drift.

## A BOON FOR BELIEVERS

Shall we simplify this to a level that we can have some fun with? Then let's give credit to Stanley Grenz, a professor of theology at Carey and Regent Colleges in Vancouver, B.C., and author of the book *A Primer on Postmodernism* (Eerdmans, 1995), who has not only helped us understand postmodernity but has used one of our favorite TV shows, *Star Trek*, to do it.

Modernism, Grenz says, is like Mr. Spock in the original *Star Trek* series. He was part-Vulcan and part-human, and always wanted to be more like his emotionless Vulcan side, more like a machine. Postmodernism is like Data, the machine in *Star Trek: The Next Generation* that wants to be human. Busters, with their emphasis on relationships, want to be more human as well.

Modernism is like Captain Kirk going out to conquer and subdue the "final frontier" of the galaxies; postmodernism is Captain Picard guiding his crew through space and helping to solve conflicts without stepping on anyone's toes. Busters have been avoiding conflict and trying to keep the peace since they were growing up in divorce-scarred homes.

The Busters are our postmodern Next Generation. And there are some definite implications for Christians because of that:

- There is no such thing as absolute truth in postmodernism. There are only choices and individual preferences. Anyone who claims to have an exclusive truth is committing an act of violence against the freedom of all.

- Busters have done away with the autonomous self and have elevated community to a higher value. They realize we can't survive alone; we need each other. Community is supposed to be one of the hallmarks of true Christians, so we have a marvelous opportunity to live out what we believe.

- Busters are searching for meaning and purpose. Postmodernism has been described as a room without walls, floor, and ceiling. Busters don't know what's up or down anymore, but within them is a compass that's searching for north, true north. Indeed, Elkind writes that pioneering French postmodernist Michel Foucalt believed that "it is not religion, as Freud claimed, that is an illusion but rather it is scientific objectivity."

- Those who don't find meaning and purpose veer toward despair. There's a lot of pain and fear within Busters because of what they've gone through. Postmodernism presents them with a bleak worldview that some Busters can't handle: The suicide rate for teens has doubled since 1968, and the number of children using drugs by the sixth grade has tripled since 1975.

- Busters have a deep-seated pessimism; they don't believe the world is, as Leibniz argued, the best of all possible worlds. Busters say: "We still can't stop wars, stamp out racism, or end child abuse. Who can? Who's even willing to try?" We need to be people who give Busters hope.

- Postmodernism produces a lack of coherence in Busters. An idea doesn't have to be logical for them to subscribe to it. That's the reason they can hold seemingly paradoxical viewpoints at the same time. If you've ever wondered why a Buster you know is gung-ho to save endangered animals and even trees while simultaneously advocating abortion, postmodernity offers a reason why. Postmodernity can produce a lot of paradoxes. What's one of the Busters' favorite phrases? "Whatever."

- Busters process truth relationally rather than propositionally. They do not respond well to intellectual apologetics. Logic is a loser. A Buster will say, "Let me see it with your life before you tell it to me with your words." Which is straight from the Bible anyway. It's how it should be. "Follow me as I follow Christ," said the apostle Paul. He called people to look at his life and see if he was practicing what he preached. We should do the same.

Postmodernity is, in our opinion, the single most powerful force in shaping the mindset, attitudes, and values of the Buster generation. A growing number of books are being written that deal with the ins and outs of this new philosophical gridwork in far greater detail than we are able to provide here. However, if we want to understand and minister to this generation, postmodernity is our starting point because from now on, the way this and following generations will look at and process truth will change the way we communicate and reason with people. The old styles of preaching and teaching will need to be modified and replaced by new approaches to telling the "old, old story."

# Chapter 5

# Nobody's Home

The world is full of emotional and spiritual orphans.
—Floyd McClung Jr.

When Sandy was a child, her best friend was her dad. They went places together. They played games together. They laughed and cuddled. But when Sandy was eight, her dad disappeared. Without a word, he left her mom and moved in with a younger girlfriend.

Sandy and her dad had little contact for the first few years. And no child support. He wasn't there to tuck her in bed anymore. He wasn't there for her birthdays. While her mom worked tirelessly to keep the household afloat, Sandy's dad had plenty of leisure time and plenty of money to spend on his girlfriend and expensive cars. Sandy's anger grew.

At twenty, Sandy is a singer. Though upbeat and bubbly among her friends, when she sings there is a plaintiveness and world-weariness in her voice from being forced to grow up too soon.

She says becoming a Christian is helping her to forgive her dad, "but every time I think about what my mom has had to go through, I get angry."

## NOT THE BRADY BUNCH

Multiply Sandy's story by the millions, and you can start to see the condition of many Busters in America. Broken and blended families have left a mark as indelible as a tattoo on the Buster psyche and heart.

About forty-six percent of the Busters are children of divorce. In *13th Gen*,[1] Strauss and Howe point out that kids born in 1968 faced three times the risk of a broken home as children born in 1948. The pervasiveness of this problem cannot be minimized. Ritchie notes that "divorce occurred on a large enough scale to be disruptive to the security of the entire generation, and to help form their earliest opinions about marriage, family and trust."[2]

The Busters grew up watching *The Brady Bunch* and *The Partridge Family*. These were picture-perfect TV families, but of course, Hollywood's blended and single-parent families were largely the product of widowhood—not divorce, which was the reality for most nontraditional families. With *The Brady Bunch*, you had not one but two widowed families coming together, having a warm, wonderful time and getting better week after week. Busters ate it up and wondered, "How come that's not my reality?" But deep down, they knew it was just a pipe dream of how they wished their families would be. For the older Busters, there was also the wistfulness produced by the nostalgic nuclear families of *Little House on the Prairie* and *The Waltons*. For the younger, *The Cosby Show* would do just fine.

Life on the viewers' side of the tube was quite different. In blended families, Busters were forced into relationships with people they didn't know and very possibly wanted nothing to do with, both stepparents and step-siblings. This leaves them ill-equipped to develop satisfying relationships. They just don't know how.

When Busters do decide to take a risk and get married, it's a different situation these days. Here's one example from real life:

A pastor sat down with an engaged couple, Colin and Marie, to discuss their plans.

"We're thinking about getting married," they said.

"Hey, that's great," the pastor said. "Tell me about your backgrounds."

"Well," began Marie, "my mother has been divorced a couple times and she's thinking about getting married again. I don't really know who my real father is."

The pastor turned to her fiance. "How about you, Colin? What was your family situation like?"

"I've got a little bit of an unusual situation," he said. "My mother is a lesbian and she lives with her lover. And I don't know who my dad is either."

The family unit has spun out in all different directions leaving the Buster generation without a place for their hearts to call "home." For an unsettling example of that, all you have to do is go to a wedding ceremony for a Buster couple. In the past, you would see the bride's family on one side and the groom's family on the other side, all in the first row. Now, the tangled web of family can extend as far as four rows back. When we've performed weddings for couples with rows of family and step-families, we see stress, frustration, weariness, and pain in the eyes of the young couple. Broken and blended families are often all they've ever known, and they are desperately searching for stability and unity at home.

## THE LATCHKEY AND DAY-CARE INITIATES

Divorce isn't the only force to shape the Buster generation's feeling of being unwanted.

We had one Buster tell us Boomers: "If it wasn't for abortion, *we* would be the biggest generation."

Even Busters who had the benefit of intact families were not immune from feeling like intrusive baggage. They were the first full-blown "latchkey children," coming home after school to a house where nobody was home. A relic of this era is a well-intentioned but downright absurdist book for latchkey kids, whose numbers doubled during the Buster era. Among other things, the book said that children who were sick and thought they might need a doctor should "carefully pick your time to talk with your parents. Remember, parents are usually exhausted when they first come home from work."[3]

To some, being "home alone," as John Hughes' blockbuster film put it, might be a pretty cool concept. But there is a great deal of fear that builds up in a child because there is a survival syndrome that develops: Don't answer the door. Don't answer the phone. Close the curtains. Call 911.

The companion to the latchkey phenomenon, of course, is day care. Whether it's a reaction to the economic forces in operation in the U.S. (which will be explored in chapter 7) or a choice of lifestyle, many households are now two-income families.

But when day care first started mushrooming among the Busters, some child-care experts thought it was a preferable alternative to stay-at-home parenting. According to Howe and Strauss, "The consensus among psychologists of that time was that away-from-home day care was beneficial for small children, that working moms (or absent dads) might be better parents than the frustrated, homebound variety."

Today, we're seeing more and more articles about moms staying home because they see what parental absence did to a generation of people.

## NO TIME FOR CHILDHOOD

We've already cited the work of David Elkind, renowned for his work in child development. A few years ago, he wrote a book called *The Hurried Child*, which influenced our thinking and that of many others. At the time, educators just gravitated toward it. Nobody called these kids "Busters" back then, but

Elkind wrote about the studies he was doing among pre-schoolers and early elementary age children. The kids were always rushed and pushed and prodded and there was never a time for them to just rest.

Looking back, it seems as if Elkind was trying to yell, "Stop! Stop! Let these kids be kids." Many Busters were expected to act like adults and think like adults at a very young age. Now, they're starting to go back and act like kids again. And now, we yell at them for not growing up.

Elkind's not the only one to feel this way. "Because of transformations in the nature of the family and in the global economy, the concept of adolescence as a preparatory stage for adulthood is essentially obsolete," writes Gaines in *Teenage Wasteland*.

Adds Karen Ritchie: "As young children, Xers sometimes found themselves cast in the role of responsible party, pragmatically scrubbing the bathroom or warming up a pizza, while the adults in their lives searched for meaningful solutions . . . or pots of gold. This was especially true when divorce entered the picture."[4]

Whether they were from broken or blended families, or were latchkey or day-care initiates, a high percentage of this generation never had the sense of support they needed, never had the chance to develop their self-image—because most of your concept of who you are is developed by your family. You need your parents and siblings to be mirrors to you, to reflect who you are and what you're expected to be.

On a more basic level, Busters have difficulty relating to people because they feel they have been betrayed by broken and blended families. They learn to distrust relationships and people in general. If you get wounded enough times early in life, you shut down, and that stops the process by which you grow as a person. As a result, Busters are a generation of people searching for their identity and trying to feel good about who they are.

## LOOKING FOR A FAMILY, LOOKING FOR A HOME

If you're like Sandy, the girl mentioned at the beginning of this chapter, how do you overcome the loss of your father? If you're reaching out to swab the wounds of a Buster from a broken or blended family, where do you begin? How do you transmit the love of God the Father to people who don't even know who their biological father is?

In his fine book *The Power of Story*, Leighton Ford writes: "Many people in this postmodern age suffer from a distorted conception of God because their earthly parents were abusive, critical, emotionally distant, or absent during their formative years."[5]

With such a viewpoint, it might seem difficult to demonstrate Christ's love to Busters. But if you look carefully at how broken and blended families have affected Busters, you begin to realize just how powerful a community of compassionate Christians can be. As we mentioned in chapter 2, the angst of this generation manifests itself in anger, aloneness, feelings of abandonment, and alienation. These characteristics have shaped Busters in the following ways:

- Above all else, Busters are searching for *security* in relationships. They don't feel safe in relationships because of their family scars. It is imperative for them that the relationships they do have remain intact regardless of the cost. This produces a fierce loyalty, which is a double-edged sword—they are apt to cling to abusive relationships as well as healthy ones.
- They are *casual, cautious,* and *curious* about relationships. They have a great deal of difficulty in developing relationships because they never saw those skills modeled. They send mixed signals: "Draw close. Stay away." If they see that you are offering them a healthy relationship and have no hidden agenda, that you honestly care about them, they will be very attracted to you

and what you are offering. But they will go slowly, and we must navigate tenderly as we reach out to them.

- They're *searching for a home* and for people to be their family. We can't stress enough that connecting to others in relationships and building a sense of community are driving forces for Busters. It's a we-centered spiritual approach, not a me-centered approach. This is a generation that longs to belong, and later in these pages we'll discuss practical ways to help this generation begin to find acceptance, healing, and love.

# Chapter 6

# The Electronic Playroom

Busters inherited junk culture. It's not our fault if we loved it—well, aspects of it.

—Nirvana

The political scientist was concerned about the influence of the media on impressionable youth: "They are picking up expressions they don't understand," he complained. "They want sixty-dollar black boots that their favorite TV star wears, and that is causing pressure on families."

A mother of two children said she felt the educational system shared the blame, and worried about the future: "I'm afraid we will be losing our traditions if this continues," she said. "The schools should step up their teachings of our history and show young people there is reason to learn your heritage and be proud of it."

But, she noted, history wasn't popular because it wasn't a hip TV show. The kids, she said, were more interested in "watching the girls on the beach in 'Baywatch.'"

Perhaps you've heard similar sentiments raised a hundred times in your family or neighborhood. But the political scientist and the mother weren't speaking to a Knight Ridder reporter about their fears for middle-class America—they were talking about the battering ram of American media that's profoundly influencing the people of their own nation, Iran. In Tehran, it's estimated that there may be as many as 200,000 satellite dishes beaming in broadcasts from around the world, or about one for every fifty residents.

The *Wall Street Journal* has written about Busters in Japan and how the older generation is worried about the attitude and motivation of the twentysomethings in their midst. And author Jianying Zha recently released a book called *China Pop: How Soap Operas, Tabloids, and Bestsellers Are Transforming a Culture.*

If such disparate societies as these are noting the influence of internal and international media on the young, there can be little doubt that Americans, who are saturated with wave upon wave of media from the day they are born, are being profoundly shaped by what they see, read, and hear. But our intent here is not to get sidetracked into the swirling debate about the lack of morality and prevalence of violence in the media, it's simply to point up the power of the media in shaping attitudes, and what implications those attitudes have in our quest to present the radical message of Jesus in a jaded age.

## THE SESAME STREET/MTV GENERATION

Busters have seen and heard it all—or at least that's the way they perceive it. They may be right. By the age of five, the leading edge of the Boomers had never even seen television. But by the time a Buster hit age five, he or she had already watched more than 5,000 hours of television.

"For many Xers," writes Karen Ritchie, "television was their baby-sitter, their entertainment, their teacher and their night-light."

In the beginning, of course, there was *Sesame Street*. Bert and Ernie and the rest of the gang descended on the airwaves in 1969 and have had a lock on them ever since.

"'Sesame Street' appeared to justify allowing a four- or five-year-old to sit transfixed in front of a television screen for unnatural periods of time," writes Neil Postman in *Amusing Ourselves to Death*. "Parents were eager to hope that television could teach their children something other than which breakfast cereal has the most crackle."[1]

Because a lot of parents worked, Busters saw more television than any generation before. *Sesame Street* is where they learned their ABCs. And MTV is where they learned—and still learn—their language and dress code. "In a typical week, four out of ten Busters (38%) view MTV, making it one of the most widely viewed television networks among Busters, and making Busters the dominant audience of that music channel," Barna says.[2]

MTV has indeed revolutionized the entertainment industry. The first video ever shown on the network was the prophetically named "Video Killed the Radio Star" by the Buggles. In the 1990s, videos are critical in the marketing of a musician, and MTV's influence has helped to launch many a career that radio had refused to take a chance on.

The videos themselves, with their impressionistic imagery and quick camera cuts from one scene to another, have been widely blamed for shortening the attention span of most Americans. Today, those rapid-fire edits can be seen in everything from 15-second TV commercials to feature films (which are sometimes directed by those who broke into the business at the helm of music videos). Yet marketing expert Ritchie sees MTV as more a symptom than a cause of a national attention deficit disorder: "Contrary to popular opinion, MTV's quick-cut, fast-fade format is attractive to Xers not because they have short attention spans but because one can see a whole segment within the confines of a network or cable commercial break."[3]

MTV's *Unplugged* series, featuring low-tech, often acoustic concerts by rock's top stars, spun off a huge new market for the music business. *Beavis and Butthead* started as a controversial MTV series and is poised to become a movie. *The Real World* put Busters together in a house for a year and taped the real-life proceedings for a highly watched series.

Even politicians can't afford to ignore the MTV viewer. In the 1992 presidential campaign, Democrat Bill Clinton courted the "Rock the Vote" generation en route to the White House. When powerful GOP House Speaker Newt Gingrich followed suit with an MTV appearance in the summer of 1995, the lesson was obvious: The *Sesame Street* generation had come of age.

## "IMAGE IS EVERYTHING"

"Image is everything," said Buster tennis star Andre Agassi. In *13th Gen* Howe and Strauss noted the reverse was true as well: If image is everything, everything is image. And image, the Busters know, can't be trusted. How can you trust an image on television or in the movies when everything from a crowd scene to the length of an actor's hair can be computer generated? How can you trust the news when they're competing for ratings and thus advertising dollars? How can you trust the printed word when the lines between newspapers and tabloids are getting a little fuzzy? How can you trust broadcasting when once-respected TV newscasts cover the same scandals and celebrities as shows like *Hard Copy* and *A Current Affair*?

"Even on news shows which provide us daily with fragments of tragedy and barbarism, we are urged by the newscasters to 'join them tomorrow.' What for? One would think that several minutes of murder and mayhem would suffice as material for a month of sleepless nights," writes Postman.

Of the newscast, he says, "The good looks and amiability of the cast, their pleasant banter, the exciting music that opens and closes the show, the vivid film footage, the attractive commercials—all these and more suggest that what we have just seen is no cause for weeping."[4]

Why weep? It's just image. While presidential hopefuls and legislators wring their hands over cinematic violence, Busters help make films like *Pulp Fiction* and *Natural Born Killers* a success with their uneasy blend of gory violence and tongue-in-cheek humor. Busters watch the world go by, but they don't believe anything they see. And they find it ironic and a bit distasteful when they see that Boomers can't make that distinction.

Simply put, Busters are media-savvy and won't allow themselves to be manipulated very easily.

"We twentysomethings . . . grew up with television and know something of the spin doctor's trade," says Steven Gibb. "We can decode the media and its attempts to market and manipulate."[5]

In *Media Virus! Hidden Agendas in Popular Culture*, prolific Buster writer Douglas Rushkoff (who is also the editor of the influential *Gen X Reader*) notes that the media is "a system with behavior as complex, far-reaching and self-sustaining as nature herself." The key to avoiding manipulation is to "seize the media," and the ready availability of technology (witness the widespread use of amateur video on newscasts) can make this possible, Rushkoff argues. Everyone can be part of the media. But is the solution really that simple?

## THE NUMBING OF AMERICA

Candidates in the 1996 presidential race, especially Kansas Senator Robert Dole, have made a grand show of linking Hollywood violence and amorality to the deterioration of American society. While the timing of their statements is suspect, they might be surprised to learn that the same Busters who packed *Pulp Fiction* are just as concerned about violence, ranking it, along with the economy, as their top concern for the society they are inheriting.

There are two reasons for this apparent paradox. The first is that Busters—raised on Atari, Nintendo, and Sega—can indeed distinguish between virtual violence and real violence. Secondly, they treat the latest bubbling violence brouhaha as a reactionary movement launched by other generations. Busters find it supremely ironic, Ritchie says, that the same generation that left them to fend for themselves in their critical adolescent years is now alarmed by the prevalence of sex, violence, and profanity in the media and its effect on the new boomlet of children.

Yet just as newscasts brightly package American carnage to keep viewers coming back, it is not a stretch to say that such frequent exposure to the worst the world has to offer can produce a numbing effect. Ask any journalist who has experienced the barrage of bad news that floods every newsroom how quickly and easily one can become calloused to the pain and tragedy of others. A hardened exterior is a coping mechanism for information overload.

What, then, of the information overload available to all in an age of satellite news reports and the dizzying world of cyberspace? Numbness becomes an equal-opportunity condition. And Busters, as we have seen, are just as cynical and skeptical as any grizzled, veteran reporter.

One other point: Being the most computer-literate and media-savvy generation on the planet poses another hazard: isolation. We all know how addictive our computer toys can be. Yet even the friendliest of electronic chat rooms can't replace the human touch, and that is what this generation ultimately lives for.

## A LOW-TECH, HIGH-TOUCH SOLUTION

Some churches that want to reach out to Busters make an understandable error. Don't people who have been raised on VCRs and computers require a multimedia blitz to get their attention? Aren't dry-ice smoke, mirrors, strobes, and videos a must if you want to speak the Busters' language? Our answer and our experience is, in a word, "no."

Yes, a church should have a respectable sound and lighting system to create a medium that Busters know, to meet stylistic expectations they have about anyone who performs on a stage.

But our experience has led us to this similar conclusion: Busters do not want to be entertained, but they will not allow themselves to be bored.

In terms of making Jesus relevant to this generation, forty-five minutes of staring at a talking head in a church service is not going to cut it. Yet they don't want a multimedia extravaganza, either. What they're looking for is not something to *entertain* them, but something to *engage* them.

In our churches, we do use contemporary forms of media to appeal to Busters, because young people are visually oriented and because we enjoy the media as well. We also use a lot of variety and spontaneity, because Busters do expect compelling stimulation—and there is nothing more compelling than the story of the Messiah, the Son of God who came to earth to sacrifice himself for our sins. But we also know that the most powerful agent of change is life-on-life sharing, and we've already alluded to it before (and will again): as Leighton Ford calls it, the "power of story."

Storytelling is perhaps the oldest form of entertainment there is and, before the advent of print and electronic media, it used to be the only way that customs, traditions, and mores were passed on from generation to generation. Today, it is no coincidence that storytelling festivals and poetry slams are enjoying great popularity, because Busters are looking for something that's a little more genuine, a little more real. It's why MTV's *Unplugged* series has become so popular, with major artists sitting on empty sets surrounded by perhaps a few candles and a small audience playing stripped-down versions of their songs. It's not Milli Vanilli, the Grammy-winning duo who admitted they weren't the ones singing on their songs and videos. It's intimate, and it's real.

Storytelling is like church *Unplugged*. It is low-tech, high-touch. And it is effective in communicating the reality of God to this postmodern generation. In fact, in this age of relativity, the value of a person's story may be the only absolute. Everyone's story is worth listening to and learning from. And here's what needs to be communicated in such a setting: "God's story intersected with my story; now I can share it with you so that you can consider making it a part of your story."

# Chapter 7

# Redefining the American Dream

Reinvent the middle class.
— Douglas Coupland, *Generation X*

Syndicated advice columnist Ann Landers was taken by surprise recently when she suggested that the reason Busters have had a hard time in today's economy was because they weren't willing to work hard like their elders. The response from young adults (yes, even they like to read Ann) was "wake up and smell the coffee," to borrow a Landers-ism. Or, as Ann put it, "Our mailroom darned near caught on fire from all the heat."

A reader from Seattle, the so-called grunge capital of the world, said:

Dear Old Battle Ax:

When did *you* last look for a job? How in the heck do you know what it's like out there? How dare you suggest that people between twenty-one and thirty miss opportunities because we are lazy.

I am fed up with people of your generation who think they are the only ones who know what hard work is. The truth is, you are growing old on *our* backs and we are going to have to shell out for pensions and medical care for people in your age group. This is not a pleasant prospect.

To be fair, there are many employers who would side with Ann. They view many Busters as young people who want to do the least amount of work for the most amount of money, who are most likely to call in sick, who want promotions immediately, who openly question supervisors' motivations, and who have little company loyalty (not that firms have much loyalty to their workers either).

In some cases, this reputation has been rooted in reality; Busters have some image restoration to undertake. But when it comes to the economy, they've just about thrown in the towel. Busters long ago sang bye-bye to the American pie. In their eyes, their predecessors got the filling and the crust, and the Busters were left with the crumbs. From their perspective, there's not much worth striving for.

Some people will try to argue that we're not in a recession, but don't try telling that to a Buster. From their viewpoint, the economy is in a downturn from which there is little hope of recovery. And economic realities play a major role in how they view the future.

Unemployment is a persistent problem among Busters, and many of those who are fortunate enough to have secured gainful employment feel like they're stuck in what Douglas Coupland called "McJobs"—something that pays the bills but has no future as a career.

When Busters look into the future, say Howe and Strauss, "they see a much bleaker vision than any of today's older generations ever saw in their own youth. Even the hard-pressed youths of the Great Depression saw a path (albeit difficult) to a bright future."[1]

Perhaps you think comparing the next generation to the youths of the Depression is a bit of a stretch. Think again. Real household income among Busters has fallen at the same rate as it did during the Depression—even more if you have kids, and the leading edge of the Busters are moving into their child-rearing years.

## $4.5 TRILLION AND COUNTING

The national debt stands at $4.5 trillion and, like a taxi to nowhere, the meter keeps running and the tab keeps growing. If Democrats and Republicans can't agree on how to balance the budget, Busters reason, how will they ever begin to pay the principal on the debt? Busters see a huge economic burden in their future.

One Buster-oriented political interest group sees it this way: "Like Wile E. Coyote waiting for a 20-ton Acme anvil to fall on his head, our generation labors in the expanding shadow of a monstrous debt."

Naturally, Busters attach the blame for this predicament to their predecessors, the Boomers, and the prosperous '80s that padded personal wallets at the expense of the future. Economist Frederick R. Strobel thinks the Busters would be right in such an assumption.

"Starting the 1980s in a creditor position—that is, with more money owed to it than it owed to other nations—the United States finished up in 1988 in just the opposite position," he writes in *Upward Dreams, Downward Mobility*.

Reaganomics, says Strobel, simply took money away from the middle and lower classes and redistributed to the uppermost income bracket, and Strobel sees an uphill struggle for those trying to make up the difference. "The most likely prospect for the near future," he says, "is that things will get far worse for middle- and lower-class America before, if ever, things get better."[2]

Busters cringe when they see the bumper sticker that says, "We're spending our kids' inheritance." They feel that's no exaggeration. The due date for paying the national debt can't be postponed forever, and they know that they're the generation who will have to pick up the tab for the credit-fueled feast of the '80s.

## WOULD YOU LIKE FRENCH FRIES WITH THAT?

Not only are there fewer Busters than Boomers to foot the bill, but there are fewer jobs as well. *Forbes* magazine reports that the sales companies listed in its Forbes 500 index have cut more than 4 million jobs in the last decade.

Busters have seen that the workplace is not a level playing field. The last documented recession that the economists agree upon began in 1990. It pushed Busters out of jobs and George Bush out of office. While about 400,000 workers older than 30 lost their jobs between May 1990 and May 1991, one million employees under 30 got the ax. Busters were the scapegoats for the recession. And when companies started hiring workers again, Busters had to turn the other cheek whether they wanted to or not.

"During previous recessions," said *Harper's,* "the majority of entry-level jobs went to recent college graduates, who were considered cheaper to hire and easier to train. After 1990, 55 percent of all new job openings went to older workers."

The jobs that do exist for Busters these days aren't exactly the cream of the crop. For every Buster making more than $30,000 a year, there are eight who make less than that figure. More and more jobs are becoming hourly-wage positions because employers are seeking to avoid having to pay for increasingly costly benefits. Pensions are drying up. And 42.8 percent of Americans between the ages of 25 and 29 don't have health insurance.

The largest employer in the U.S. is Manpower Inc., the temporary-job agency. The largest and fastest growing labor sector is the service industry, which is known for short-term employment and relatively low wages.

All their lives, Busters have heard the party line: "If you do well in high school, and work hard in college to achieve your degree, you'll gain entry to your career field of dreams."

But that dream has become something resembling a nightmare. Since 1989, corporate recruiting on college campuses has plummeted by 47 percent. Many college grads find themselves as assistant managers working the drive-through window at fast-food restaurants, driving UPS trucks, or making change as they sit caged within bullet-proof glass booths at self-serve gas stations. All the while, they wait for an opportunity that may never come in their chosen field .

## THE POWER OF PERSONAL PLASTIC

The *Los Angeles Times* has called the Busters the "have-nots," and that's an appropriate designation. Most of the Busters grew up in relative affluence. "Since we grew up in the '80s, we had all our toys," a Midwest college junior named Mark told us.

But now that they're on their own, the prosperity is gone. "Anyone who can't obtain at age 30 the same amenities he enjoyed at age 15 has plenty of reason to obsess over dollars and cents," noted Howe and Strauss wryly.

The greed personified by Gordon Gekko, Michael Douglas's character in the movie *Wall Street*, is a pretty accurate assessment of how Busters view the '80s. As role models go, it was a poor example. But many Busters, faced with a less-than-perfect present and an even grimmer future, have embraced the power of plastic with a cry of *Carpe diem!* ("Seize the day!"). They live for the now—they'd rather not even think about what faces them in the future. "We still have that adolescent mortality complex," said Mark, "where you think you'll never get old and have to deal with that."

One recent study has suggested that Busters are saving more money than Boomers. We haven't seen that in our experience. We know many Busters who are tens of thousands of dollars in debt, an albatross that will take them a good ten years to get out from under. Auto dealerships used to be one of the few places that would offer young people credit, often enticing them with "recent graduate rebates" and other sales gimmicks. Today, Busters are a prime target of the corporate credit-card clan. Some Busters, like Mark, use the new breed of bank debit cards which only allow them to purchase items they have the savings to back up, but many others get buried by the lure of easy debt.

If you add to that the college loans incurred as Busters pursue the bachelor's degree that the business world says they must possess to have even a sliver of a chance at a job in their field of choice, you begin to see a problem with serious ramifications. Says *Forbes*: "Generation Xers have no hang-ups about going into debt. They have been brought up on credit cards, and over 60 percent of this age group's college students took out student loans; the average graduate owed over $8,000."

We have had to teach some Busters how to balance a checkbook. It's that basic. And that scary.

## THE BIG SQUEEZE

On Mark's campus, the joke goes like this: Boomers going through the Social Security system is like a large mouse going through a boa constrictor's body. It's wider than the snake's body, but the snake has to make it fit anyway.

If personal debt is ominous for the Busters, paying for the Boomers' Social Security is beyond description. Just do some simple math. Take 46 million Busters, and tax them enough to pay for the retirement of 74 million Boomers, who are more affluent than the Busters to begin with. Next, add in the factor of the so-called Blasters, the baby boomlet produced by many Boomers who delayed childbearing (and a few young Buster parents as well). Then, tax the Busters some more to pay for the Blasters' schools.

Oh, you say, aren't Busters unlikely to own homes and thus pay the property taxes from which most school funding comes? Guess again. Even if older adults own most of the property, you can bet that they'll pass along property-tax costs in the rental price. Plus, there's a grass-roots movement afoot that would fund education through income tax, not property tax.

Got that equation figured? To Busters, it adds up to a big squeeze enforced by the older and younger generation.

In a July 1995 study by Rand, the California think tank, economists said the gap between the rich and the poor in the U.S. continues to widen and that the Social Security system will have a hard time delivering on its promises. That's hardly a surprise to Busters, who believe the well will be dry by the time their turn at retirement comes around. In fact, the political advocacy group Third Millenium said one of its surveys shows that more Busters believe in UFOs than believe any FICA tax residuals will be around for them at age sixty-five.

As for assembling 401K plans and IRAs for themselves, most Busters are hard-pressed enough to survive today—they have nothing left for tomorrow.

## REDEFINING THE AMERICAN DREAM

According to George Barna, fifty-three percent of Busters still live with their parents. Fifty-seven percent say they'll never be able to afford a home. And fifty-four percent say they'll never achieve financial security.

Their saving grace financially may be their familiarity with technology, something their elders have yet to come to grips with. As Mark jokes, "We're more competent. We're more comfortable with technology. A generation that can't even program the clocks on their VCRs shouldn't be allowed to govern. It's as simple as that."

But technology won't make Busters rich, and they know it. That's why work is merely a means to an end. That is why they're often apathetic and angry. And it is why they're redefining the American Dream.

The American Dream is an invisible but very real dividing line between the generations. The question for Busters is not only "Can I achieve the American Dream of a good salary, a nice car, and a split-level suburban home," but also "Do I want to achieve that?"

The answer is that most Busters believe that the traditional American Dream is beyond their grasp. Plus, they have watched some Boomers destroy their relationships and families while climbing the corporate ladder. To Busters, owning expensive cars and homes doesn't matter as much as enjoying life and developing satisfying relationships.

Busters are fashioning a new American Dream: to be whole and to live in harmony with other people and their surroundings. A career is merely the survival mechanism that allows them to pursue the deeper things in life; it's not the end in itself.

To be more specific, Busters want to experience community and they want to make a difference. It's not that they necessarily want to make a difference for themselves; they want to make the world a better place for their kids. They don't want their kids to go through what they went through. They're the "fix-it" generation, remember?

Redefining the American Dream is a wonderful thing, because what Busters are putting as their top priority is relationships. While it's true that Busters seem ill-equipped to forge healthy relationships, that can be an area in which we can reach out to them. Because to Busters, relationships are more important than achievements. People are more important than possessions. Grass-roots involvement and volunteerism is more important than looking out for number one. But don't expect Busters to form a national coalition to save Rwanda or Bosnia or whatever nation is mired in the crisis of the moment. They're more apt to help one person on their block or in their neighborhood.

Serving other people is Busters' way of restoring their world and bringing some wholeness to themselves as well. It's like the old story about the child and the map:

A father was trying to take an afternoon nap, but his child kept interrupting him, kept trying to get him to stay awake. Finally, the father noticed a page of the newspaper lying on the floor. The page featured a map of the world, and the father tore it into many pieces.

"I'll tell you what," he told the child. "I need to get some sleep, but I'd love to play with you a little later. Go ahead and put this puzzle of the world together, and when you're done, wake me up and we'll play."

"Okay," said the child.

The father thought he'd get at least an hour of shut-eye, but ten minutes later the child was shaking him awake, showing him a map of the world that was perfect in every way.

"Why, that's incredible," the father gasped. "How did you get that put together so fast?"

"It was easy, Dad," the child said. "See? On the other side of the page was a picture of a person. Once I put my person together, the world looked just fine."

And that is how the Busters of the world hope to heal their world—by finding healing for themselves and their peers, one person at a time. It's our mission to help them do just that.

# Part 3

A Hunger for Purpose

# Chapter 8
# Let's Get Spiritual

Music is the kids' religion.

—Donna Gaines

If you want to learn about the Busters, try tuning in to their culture. Try listening to an alternative-rock station. Grunge, the Seattle sound full of muddy guitar feedback and anguished vocals, has faded from the scene but, as we noted earlier, the Buster generation is more of an attitude than an exacting demographic, and that nonconformist attitude has spread throughout the music industry, regardless of genre.

If there is a Generation X anthem, it may be the sound of Pearl Jam's Eddie Vedder wailing "Not For You." Ironically, one opportunistic radio station borrowed the song title "This is not for you" as an advertising slogan, only to earn a rebuke in concert from Vedder, whose displeasure echoed Coupland's contention that "I am not a target market."

Pearl Jam may be the most popular band in the land, but rarely have a generation's deepest feelings and attitudes been so vividly chronicled by a plethora of artists. If you tune in to one of those stations, you'll hear about everything from numbness and alienation ("Hurt" by Nine Inch Nails), sour relationships ("Loser" by Beck), cynicism ("Feeling Good" by Jennifer

Trynin), and pain ("Every Generation's Got Its Own Disease" by Fury in the Slaughterhouse).

For while Busters can be a bit guarded in person, they've learned quickly and effectively to use cultural expression as an outlet for their emotions. Busters' feelings are usually bubbling just below the surface. They may feel at ease uncorking their joy and sorrow anonymously in an online chat room. But the artists of their generation help them verbalize their fears and hopes, and those of us who are trying to better understand Busters have found music to be a true touchstone.

Why do Busters feel this way? Because of the forces we outlined in part 2. They feel betrayed; they feel there is no one and nothing they can trust.

## THE SEARCH VIA CULTURE

The impact of culture upon Busters cannot be underestimated. Their lives revolve around music and visuals; they account for half the tickets sold at movie theaters and spend more on music via concerts, CDs, and tapes than all other age groups combined. For a generation that doesn't have a lot of disposable income, those facts speak volumes. Thus, what's contained in those music and visuals speaks volumes as well about the Busters.

The new brand of rock, writes Sarah Ferguson, "is music for kids who grew up too fast. They keep reaching back for a childhood denied."[1]

Busters find various ways to deal with that loss of innocence and, as the arts reflect, nihilism is a primary outlet. The TV movie *Zooman*, for example, took its title and theme from the label that some African-Americans apply to individuals in their community with absolutely no moral standards at all.

The art film *Kids* is a documentary-like cautionary tale against AIDS, featuring graphic depiction of city teens whose world consists almost exclusively of drug use and sexual conquest.

In music, drugs and sex have been intertwined with rock 'n' roll from its beginnings. Drug use is on the upswing today, with references to heroin and marijuana use surfacing in lyrics. Many of the songs, as we have seen, are songs of searching. But we wouldn't necessarily put the increase in drug use among teens as evidence of a search. In the '60s, drugs were seen as a means of exploration, of expanding your mind. But today, we contend that drugs are used more for a numbing effect. Many Busters are hurting and are tired of feeling the pain. It's nihilistic; if you believe there is no future to live for, why not do drugs?

The "just do it" credo is more than a pitch for an athletic apparel company; it's a mindset prevalent among people who have "no fear," to borrow another modern catchphrase, of anything, including AIDS. It's why *Rolling Stone* nicknamed Busters the "latex generation" for their casual attitude toward sexual partners. Society—and Christianity—is quick to condemn such symptoms without a glance at, or a prescription for, the underlying cause. But we see this nihilism as a desperate plea for community, for emotional intimacy.

Busters are indeed searching, though most would tell you they're not sure what the object of their quest is, beyond peace of mind. In *Life After God*, Coupland traces that search from the Busters' childhood innocence to adult skepticism:

> Life was charmed but without politics or religion. It was the life of children of the pioneers—life after God—a life of earthly salvation on the edge of heaven. Perhaps this is the finest thing to which we may aspire, the life of peace, the blurring between dream life and real life—and yet I find myself speaking these words with a sense of doubt.
>
> I think there was a trade-off somewhere along the line. I think the price we paid for our golden life was an inability to fully believe in love; instead we gained an irony that scorched everything it touched. And I wonder if this irony is the price we paid for the loss of God.[2]

In moments of secret and silence, all that surface brashness that the world sees as the Buster image falls away. And young people reflect on their search and wonder if God exists and what such a Being must be like.

## THE SEARCH FOR COMMUNITY

In an article entitled "The Comfort of Being Sad," Sarah Ferguson describes the pathos of a homeless teen named Bones. Bones's numerous tattoos trace the path he has taken in life, and it is nothing if not a search for meaning: from skinhead to heroin addict to born-again Christian to skatepunk to acid-head to a chef's assistant. As Bones moves from town to town, his primary constant is his battered backpack, with a weathered doll of the *Sesame Street* character Ernie flopping around from atop the backpack.[3] What was it that Ferguson said about "reaching back for a childhood denied"?

Bones may be a bit of an extreme, but Busters are a spiritually hungry group. No longer enamored, as some Boomers have been, by the promised Nirvana brought about by scientific and technological advances, they're looking for an ultimate purpose. For them that means a group purpose—a unifying force that pulls us all together.

This is indeed a change from the individualism of the modern era and the Boomer generation, writes Gaines. "Our national preoccupation with psychotherapy and the 'inner life' of the individual has blinded us to other ways of seeing. The collective, the sociological, has been conspicuously absent from the narrative."[4]

Busters say the people who have the most influence on their values are their friends and peers. We've seen firsthand that many Busters make decisions based on what their group thinks. Previous generations tend to operate more autonomously. "Postmodern people are not only hungry for empowerment," says Leighton Ford. "They are also hungry for community, for a sense of fellowship with Someone or Something larger than themselves."[5]

The world at large inherently sees the value in this. From support groups to "Star Trek" conventions to jitterbug dance clubs, people of common interests and values enjoy coming together and bonding. Many plan their schedules around such activities.

One good example of the kind of community Busters are yearning for is the highly regarded Kerrville Folk Festival in Texas, which has been going strong for twenty-five years. The festival lasts a whopping eighteen days, and people come from all over the world to listen to musicians ranging from folk statesman Peter Yarrow to critically acclaimed Butch Hancock to local artists. But when the concerts end at midnight, the festival really begins. The campfires light up the Quiet Valley Ranch and musicians well-known and obscure, professional and amateur, gather around the crackling flames to pass around a guitar and share their songs with each other for as long as their voices hold out.

The camaraderie and community that pervades the grounds for the better part of two and a half weeks is threatening to some festival-goers. "Everybody just comes up and starts talking to you like they know you," grumbled one visitor to a Fort Worth Star-Telegram reporter. "It's too strange for me." But for many others, that's exactly why they keep coming back year after year. "Maybe it's just the way the world ought to be," said one enthusiast. "The festival is, maybe, the perfect definition of 'community.' Everybody takes care of everybody else. You walk in and think, 'Hey, I just came home.'"

A sense of home. A sense of family. A fellowship. That is what we pray and work and strive for in our churches. That is what real Christianity is supposed to be all about. But that is not what comes to mind for Busters when they think about the church. In the next chapter, we'll look at Busters' perceptions and Christian reality.

# Chapter 9

# Walls and Bridges: How Busters View the Church

This is my commandment, that you love one another
as I have loved you.

—Jesus in John 15:12

A year ago, Diane was a student at a prestigious college, one of
the few campuses that still experiences some intensive corporate recruiters from the Fortune 500. In one of her sociology
classes, the course included a section on how religion and
people's beliefs shape the way they perceive the American dream.

As the class discussed various religions, from Buddhism to
Islam to Hinduism, the students "were very open," remembers
Diane. "They were accepting of everything."

But when the topic was Christianity, the mood in the room
suddenly changed.

"They were making fun of it," says Diane, who was raised
as a Catholic and became an evangelical Christian in her freshman year of college. "It went on and on. People were very negative about it. So finally I had to say something."

"This really disturbs me," Diane told her classmates. "No
one here really wants to hear about this, and it's something I've
invested with my entire life."

A friend named Rick was the next to speak.

"We're sorry, Diane," he said. "I think we're laughing out of ignorance. It's easier to laugh than admit that we're ignorant about it."

To Busters, religion is relative. Barna's research indicates one-third of Busters believe that people of all religions pray to the same God, regardless of what they call him or her. And while *13th Gen* notes that forty-two percent of teenagers say they frequently pray alone, they still say that friends, home, school, and media have greater influence on their lives than religion.

On the West Coast, we have seen many Busters wearing crystals or other New Age and Eastern symbols. They're very interested in spiritual things; they're just not necessarily interested in Christian concepts. But it's something they generally keep hidden deep beneath the surface of their psyche. Writes Coupland:

> Now—here is my secret: I tell it to you with an openness of heart that I doubt I shall ever achieve again, so I pray that you are in a quiet room as you hear these words. My secret is that I need God—that I am sick and can no longer make it alone. I need God to help me give, because I no longer seem to be capable of giving; to help me be kind, as I no longer seem capable of kindness; to help me love, as I seem beyond being able to love.[1]

## STAINED-GLASS STEREOTYPES

Coupland and the Busters are not resistant to spiritual matters. They're not resistant to the concept of God. But they are resistant to the Christian church. They view the church as being separatist, segregated, institutional, irrelevant, judgmental, holier-than-thou, controlling, authoritarian. And to some degree, they're right.

To be fair, churches run by Boomers and others tend to be highly organizational in structure and very cause-oriented, which are values that the Busters simply don't embrace.

But some of the Busters' perceptions are secondhand. They are the first generation that has had very little exposure to any kind of church; it was during the Busters' formative years that the exodus from mainline denominations began to occur.

Since their perceptions are not based on experience—and we've hammered away in these pages about how Busters will trust nothing unless they've experienced it—the good news is that these perceptions can change by exposure to authentic Christianity, the "attractive power of Christian community, the fellowship of the Holy Spirit," as Leighton Ford describes it. If these preconceptions about Christianity were formed by hearsay, by their parents, or by friends who went off the deep end in an unbalanced way, a vibrant Christian community can shatter that stained-glass stereotype.

## MULTIPLYING, NOT DIVIDING

Busters see Christianity as a divisive faith. They see it as the haves and the have-nots, the insiders and the outsiders. Busters are culturally sensitive people. They're the ones who want to break down all traces of dividing lines. We have to help them understand that's what Christianity is all about—reuniting estranged humans with each other and with their Creator. In one sense, of course, Jesus is exclusive and dogmatic. The other religions say, "We're all one." Jesus said, "I am the way, the truth, and the life." But he invited everyone to come to him. Jesus doesn't want anyone to be left out. His goal is not division; it is to multiply his blessings of peace, inclusion, affirmation, and acceptance to everyone—the very qualities that a Buster seeks.

Still, Busters are not always drawn to messages that claim to be "true." Inclusiveness and community are values they cherish more than truth. To them, the truth is neither real nor objective. What's real to Busters is what they experience, and what they want to experience is a sense of community. Somehow, we need to communicate Jesus' message more effectively.

Busters view Eastern religions as being process-oriented. In these faiths, you're continually becoming a better person. Remember the TV show *Kung Fu*? David Carradine was evolving each week as the young man his mentor called "Grasshopper." Busters see Eastern faiths as something allowing them the time and space in a chaotic world to process their experiences in order to attain a higher state of betterment, of consciousness. It's an affirmation of where they are. And it doesn't mean you're not already good or even better than that when you first begin the process; you're just becoming better. It's always easier to think of yourself as already being good than as a person who makes mistakes and is in need of mercy and grace.

## PASSAGE TO WHOLENESS

Curiously, when we interact with people who are searching, we find they're often a little frustrated with the Eastern faiths. There's no rite of passage by which they can say, "How do I know where I stand? How do I know how far I've come?" It's like a continuum, and the people we talk with say they recognize that they have a need for boundaries built into them.

This rite of passage is not only a spiritual issue but a maturity issue. The bar mitzvah is a Jewish boy's doorway into adulthood. Many African and Third World cultures have their own initiation rites. In fact, an American-educated Burkina Faso scholar suggests that one of the problems facing young people in the U.S. today is the lack of a rite of passage, an omission that, if corrected, might make a dent in the gang problem.

We need to communicate quite clearly that Jesus is the way; he is our rite of passage. And with that entrance into a new lifestyle comes his promise of eternal life as well. That is a security that is not guaranteed in the other faiths.

## LURE OF THE EAST

With such a powerful message, how has the church gotten sidetracked? When Busters look at the church, they see more roadblocks and detours than access points or paths to empowerment. It's like road-construction season. And again, when we look at the church from their perspective, we have to agree. The responsibility is on the shoulders of Christians to build bridges and become guides for Busters on their spiritual journey, for the competition is getting fierce and brazen.

Given the stereotypes about Christianity, it's easy to see why Busters are attracted to New Age practices. There's the promise of a better life, the promise of a faith that's inclusive, the environmental aspect of concepts like harmonic convergence and Gaia. Eastern religions are attractive because of what some of the faith systems promise. "Being at peace," for example, is a Zen concept. But perhaps most importantly, Eastern religions make few moral demands on people. Christianity goes against the grain or our fallen human nature; in general, Eastern faiths view humanity as imbued with goodness and getting better all the time.

What we notice is that there is a syncretism movement going on. In many cases, Christianity will be just one part of many parts that makes up a Buster's spirituality. It's a build-your-own-religion phenomenon. We can't begin to count the number of times we've heard people speak of the New Age concepts of "being aligned," "being centered," or "finding peace within yourself." Their search may include a little bit of Buddhism and Hinduism, a cupful of Castaneda, a teaspoon of Taoism. This is true of many Boomers as well, but the trend is more extensive among Busters.

Yet we need to be very careful not to try to communicate the Christian message at the expense of other faith systems. Sometimes, we get off on a tangent of "proving" Christianity by attempting to "disprove" Islam or Hinduism. That's just going to be a land mine of intolerance for a diversity-sensitive Buster.

"Aha," the Buster will say. "The stereotype is true. You really are narrow-minded and judgmental."

When discussing spiritual issues with Busters, we have found it most helpful to focus on Jesus. Because of their lineage of inner turmoil and pain, we have found that Busters identify intimately with the suffering of Jesus:

> He was despised and rejected by men, a man of sorrows, and familiar with suffering. Like one from whom men hide their faces he was despised, and we esteemed him not. (Isaiah 53:3)

The Cross is a powerful testimony and symbol to Busters, and we have found that the two-edged sword of Scripture is quite adept at slashing through the inconsistencies of Eastern tenets and piercing Busters' hearts. But this biblical blade remains sharp only as long as the testimony of our lives backs it up.

## SHATTERING STEREOTYPES

Busters are not going to listen to your words as much as they are going to observe your life. That's why it's so strategic for you to develop a relationship with them. The thing that's going to speak most powerfully to them is the way you live your life: "Do you really act out what you say you believe?"

We must learn to let the Bible speak through our lives.

A Buster survey commissioned by Willow Creek Community Church shows Christians have a long way to go to change the next generation's perceptions about Christianity. The church, according to Busters, "is old, traditional, and behind the times. If it was caring, it is not anymore. Now it is just trying to bring in money." Buster men in particular see churches as "pushy, uniform, and dead."

Busters aren't coming to church because they see it more as walls than bridges. They don't think the church wants them, and there's no reason for them to think otherwise. Their pic-

ture of Christianity can be anything from a TV evangelist beg-
ging for money to the psychopath that Robert DeNiro portrayed in the movie *Cape Fear*, who goes around exacting
revenge in the name of Christianity.

Many Busters see the church as a castle surrounded by a
moat; and the people inside are not interested in lowering the
drawbridge. That's a perception we need to change. Not only
do we need to lower the drawbridge, but we must demonstrate
to this new generation that we welcome them into our
churches and ministries, so they can explore who Jesus is as
they observe how we worship, serve, and seek to follow him
with our lives.

It's been said that Christianity is always one generation
away from extinction. In light of that compelling truth, it is
imperative that we prayerfully and creatively work at changing
the perceptions of people like Diane's classmates. In part 4,
we'll offer some of the ideas that we have used to do just that.

# Part 4

## Transforming the Next Generation

# Chapter 10

# The Four R's: A Buster Primer

Let's just hope we accidentally build God.
—Douglas Coupland

Linda's family has had a tumultuous spiritual life over the years. She grew up in a Christian home and her mother in particular was a strong and steadying influence in her life.

"My mother was a strong role model for me," she says. "She was a woman who really walked the road of faith."

But Linda's brother Barry wasn't quite as fortunate in that department. "Barry never had that from my dad," Linda says. "It's kind of sad; he got the raw end of the deal. My dad portrayed himself as the spiritual head of the household, but all through our lives, he wasn't that at all."

When Linda went off to college, her faith was tested. "I went through the toughest issues in college," she says. "I was a really straight kid growing up, but in college I started running with the wrong crowd."

It was at that point that some friends encouraged her to investigate a local evangelical church that had a "church within a church" specifically for Busters.

"It's neat to look around and see 450 people your age there. That church was a godsend for me," she says, especially when her parents started going through the process of a divorce while she was there. Linda got involved with the Buster church and would lend her vocal talents to the services, singing everything from Christian pop songs to secular rock tunes to even a song from the Broadway hit *Les Miserables* that addressed some spiritual issues.

Linda saw her life (and some of her friends' lives) turn around at the Buster church. "When I graduated," she says, "I was able to stand in front of the church and sing and give my testimony. I told them how I felt a place of safety there. I had the freedom to be sad or angry. The church kind of became my family."

Barry, meanwhile, is still struggling. "He's wandered very far away from the Lord," Linda says. "He'll get involved in some mess and then go to church once or twice, and then he's back in another mess. My parents' divorce has affected him more than he thinks. He's really searching."

Barry isn't alone. We hope it is clear that this is no small search going on in Busters' hearts for purpose and meaning. Douglas Coupland describes his own search—and perusal of Christianity—in *Life After God:*

> And there were Christian radio stations, too, so many many stations, and the voices on them seemed so enthusiastic and committed. They sounded like they sincerely believed in what they were saying, and so for once I decided to pay attention to these stations, trying to figure out what exactly it was they were believing in, trying to understand the notion of Belief.[1]

What motivated him to listen? Their enthusiasm and sincerity. But it heads south from there:

> The radio stations all seemed to be talking about Jesus nonstop, and it seemed to be this crazy orgy of projection, with everyone projecting onto Jesus the antidotes to the things that had gone wrong in their own lives. He is Love. He is Forgiveness. He is Compas-

sion. He is a Wise Career Decision. He is a Child Who Loves Me.... I did not deny that the existence of Jesus was real to these people—it was merely that I was cut off from their experience in a way that was never connectable.[2]

Coupland is saying, "I see your mouth moving, I can hear your words, but there's a distance between you and me. Even though I can say I understand you, I'm still not able to buy into your belief because there's this distance—we're not connecting."

Sometimes, Busters (like Coupland) feel as if they're in an alien culture when they encounter Christians. They're partly right. Christians often use many terms that are difficult for others to understand. We sometimes expect people who are spiritual seekers to enter the Christian subculture unaided by even a translator as they search for meaning and purpose. But in reality, we have found it helps immeasurably when we are active in the culture at large using the language they're comfortable with as we encourage them to consider the claims of Christ. And Busters have a language and background quite different from previous generations.

## ACROSS THE CULTURES

Reaching out to Busters is very much like going to a completely different country and immersing yourself in a foreign culture. If we were going to China and wanted to reach out to the people of a rural village, we would go live among them, learn their language, build relationships, and work to discover what kind of redemptive analogies we could find in their culture to communicate the message of the Cross to them. That is what we must do if we hope to make Jesus relevant to Busters.

When you take a look at chapter 17 in the book of Acts, you'll find that what we're up against is nothing new. Paul encountered the same difficulty communicating to a different culture in Athens, and this chapter is a microcosm of our dilemma as well as an example of our opportunity: "While Paul was waiting for them in Athens, he was greatly distressed to see that the city was full of idols" (verse 16). Paul spent time reasoning with them in the synagogues and he caught the attention of the philosophers of that area—he had some lively debates with them. Then, in verses 22 and 23, "Paul then stood up in the meeting of the Areopagus and said: 'Men of Athens! I see that in every way you are very religious. For as I walked around and looked carefully at your objects of worship, I even found an altar with this inscription: TO AN UNKNOWN GOD. Now what you worship as something unknown I am going to proclaim to you.'"

What do we see here as a model of evangelism in Paul? First of all, he could say to these people, "I see that in every way you are very religious." He affirmed their seeking, he affirmed their search. "For as I walked around and looked carefully ..."—he understood what they were worshiping and how they were worshiping. He didn't just come in with his message. He took time to understand what was going on inside of them and what their religious endeavors had consisted of up to that point. And he takes their search and he brings the Gospel into it.

Once he understood them, what were some of the key elements of Paul's approach? First of all, it was *real*, it was raw. Paul didn't try to impress them with fancy words, but there could be no mistaking his sincerity. The Athenians called Paul a "babbler" (verse 18), and Paul himself admitted he was not "a trained speaker." Secondly, Paul's approach was *rousing*. When he affirmed their search and proclaimed an "unknown god" to them, he roused their interest.

Next, he spoke to them on a topic that was highly *relevant* to them. The Athenians enjoyed "talking about and listening to the latest ideas" (verse 21). Paul's proclamation of the Gospel was such a new concept that they actually asked Paul to explain it to them.

Finally, Paul's approach was *relational.* Just as had happened in Paul's other journeys, some of his listeners rejected him. But others told him, "We want to hear you again on this subject" (verse 32). It took time; it always takes time to build relationships, but that is usually where the greatest impact is made.

So how do we connect with the Busters and Athenians of our world in a way that they can understand? In reaching Busters, the aforementioned four elements are essential. In the school of Buster communication, there aren't three R's, there are four.

## THE FIRST R: REAL

First of all, your communication has got to be *real.* With a generation that is so skeptical because "image is everything," you have to work diligently to be real with them. What we mean by real is vulnerable, transparent, imperfect. Real, in our minds, is akin to raw. Like Paul, it's unpolished. This may be a reaction to the force of the media, which Busters see as anything but real. It takes a big person to be able to admit personal flaws and imperfections to others, because there's something inside us that takes care of image protection. We strongly identify with Paul in the fourth chapter of 2 Corinthians where he talks about how the treasure of Christ is contained in earthen vessels.

Earthen vessels refers to ordinary, cracked, everyday pottery. And why is this treasure contained in this mundane pottery? So that no one would become so enamored with the pottery that they would miss the treasure. We find that Christians demonstrate their authenticity when they say, "I'm going to quit pretending that this piece of pottery called my life is perfect. I'm going to start letting the treasure of the Gospel show through the cracks in my life."

Steve, the pastor of a vibrant Buster church, and his wife stumbled onto this concept in their ministry during a time of great inner turmoil.

"We were experiencing some problems in our marriage," he acknowledges. "It got to the point one weekend where I stood before the church and said, 'I need to tell you about what's going on in my life.'"

In a sensitive way, he shared some very personal, difficult issues and said, "You know, sometimes I really wonder if I'm qualified to be your pastor. But you need to know what's going on, and Christ is helping us through this period."

Steve thought they would lose a good portion of the people in the church at that point. He thought they would walk out and say, "If he doesn't have his life together, we want no part of him—and this church." But just the opposite happened.

"People," adds Steve, "came up to us—many of them weren't married—and said, 'I deal with those kinds of fears, too.' And people with very little exposure to church, people who were just kind of checking us out and investigating Christianity, started coming up to me and saying, 'Let me tell you what's going on inside of me.' It was an amazing response. But because I went out on a limb and tried to be as open and real as I could be, it established an environment where people said, 'If he's willing to trust me so much that he's leaving himself wide open and vulnerable like that, I'm going to try trusting him a little bit and see what happens.'"

When you're real with people, you gain their trust because you took the first risk. In being real, Steve's story made an impact on his postmodern listeners. They could identify with his relational struggles because many of them had come from families with a variety of troubles.

## THE SECOND R: ROUSING

As Steve's experience shows, trust is one of the Busters' big issues. How does trust occur? How do you build trust with a generation that's experienced a lot of wounds? Simply by taking the first step in vulnerability.

Thus, the second element in communicating to a Buster is that it must be *rousing*. We like that term because it's an old English hunting word that refers to how the dogs would flush out the fox or flush out the pheasant from its hiding place. A secondary meaning is "to awaken from slumber." In our dealings with Busters, we mean that there's something concealed that needs to be brought out from its hiding place, or there's someone who needs to be awakened to spiritual realities.

Busters may be sitting before you at a meeting, or they may be in a one-on-one situation with you, but you can safely make a basic assumption that they are in hiding or slumbering. They may not know this themselves—it may even be on a subconscious level—but they're often covering something up. They're protecting themselves, and we need to think through how we can encourage them to stop hiding so that they can find a place of healing.

If this sounds paradoxical, it is, but postmodern Busters are full of paradoxes. They expect realness from others, but the fact that they're hiding does indeed imply that, at least in certain areas, they are being less than real themselves. Perhaps one reason they find such authenticity appealing is because it's a quality that they aspire to.

There are no magic formulas for rousing Busters. We just know some of the things that we've done to encourage this process to take place.

For instance, New Song did a series called "Great Sex." This included "The Great Gift of Sex," which explained how God created sex and that he wants us to enjoy it. That was a new concept for Busters; they often think that God is antisex. Another topic was "The Great Divide," on why God doesn't want people to be sexually involved before marriage—you could have heard a pin drop during that one. For "The Great Frustration," Dieter and his wife spoke about how, in their early years of marriage, their sexual relationship was frustrating.

That series brought a lot of people out of hiding. It showed them that here was a church that was willing to talk about something that really mattered to them and share it in a forthright, vulnerable manner.

Homosexuality was also dealt with in that series. There's a crucial topic for this age group. A young man at New Song was slowly moving out of that lifestyle, and he wrote a letter that described how he felt when he first started coming to church as a homosexual seeking after God. That letter was the basis for a monologue performed by a New Song actor. It was, again, an approach that shattered stained-glass stereotypes because it came at the audience from a direction that they didn't expect.

Using someone's genuine, honest experience effectively roused people willingly from their hiding place. But how do you follow up something like that? In this case, with a song that expressed God's compassion for people involved in things that may not please him, and how he still is reaching out to them nonetheless.

## THE THIRD R: RELEVANT

Busters are a pragmatic generation. Howe and Strauss, the authors of *13th Gen*, say, "Above all else, religion must be useful in order for them to listen to it." We need to continually think about how this is going to intersect with their life.

The third element is that when you communicate to Busters, it must be *relevant* to their generation. Busters have different questions: What does the Bible say about the environment? What does the Bible say about racism? What does the Bible say about reconciliation? They want to know if the Bible is still relevant today. These are issues that anyone—not just a pastor—can discuss.

During our services, we attempt to communicate cultural relevance to media-savvy Busters by using contemporary music and film clips to create an atmosphere of common ground.

But when we are trying to communicate the relevance of Christianity, we also do it as we share how God is helping us in what is going on in our lives. As Howe and Strauss said, "Does it work?" If we don't have examples of that in our own life, we probably have not been paying attention. Perhaps we've taken for granted the numerous times God helped us through a difficult situation on the job or in a relationship.

That relevance is what is going to get behind the boredom and the apathy you're going to encounter when you're dealing with Busters who have been burned by the church or simply have no interest in traditional Christianity. The realness that will overwhelm their circuitry, their postmodern worldview, is when someone like Sandy, the young woman mentioned in chapter 5 who harbors anger toward her wayward father, is courageous enough to share her story. It's not a pastor or someone in authority outlining how we should live our lives. It's one of them, one of us, opening her heart, taking a risk to be real and relevant in a way that is also rousing. Yes, Jesus has turned her life around. But that doesn't mean her life is perfect, that she doesn't experience pain or struggle.

We need to see ourselves as fellow strugglers. When a person like Sandy seizes the initiative to take a risk and tell you something about her own life when she's not sure how you're going to respond to it, that's a key to unlock and unburden hearts. It's as if she is saying, "You may laugh at me, you may mock me, you may think worse of me, but I'm willing to be vulnerable. And when I take that risk, you're going to be in a much better position to take a risk with me as well."

## THE FOURTH R: RELATIONAL

The first three R's inevitably pour into the fourth aspect of Buster ministry: it must be *relational*.

Relationships, of course, is a big buzzword for Busters. In our experience, one way we have tried to communicate the relevance of Jesus is by not only offering premarital counseling but dating counseling. It has been called The Great Date Race. Or Checkmates. And it's been very successful.

Busters are eager to learn how to relate to each other, because that's a life skill they frequently had little contact with as they grew up. They want to avoid the pitfalls they saw their parents blunder into. People who've had little or no exposure to Christianity say dating counseling had a great effect on them. Usually a boyfriend or girlfriend brings them. Dating is an extremely relevant topic and a place to stake some common ground; the seminar develops the skills needed to build healthy relationships, and it offers an environment where people can be real with each other. It's reaching people through relationships.

You've seen the word *relational* a lot in these pages. We think more and more evangelism is going to happen through relationships. The Gospel is going to be communicated more incarnationally than propositionally or cognitively.

A poem was sent to us at Willow Creek by a seeker who communicated the importance of being real in relationships.

Do you know
do you understand
that you represent
Jesus to me?

Do you know
do you understand
that when you
treat me with gentleness,
it raises the question in my mind
that maybe He is gentle, too.
Maybe He isn't someone
who laughs when I am hurt.

Do you know
do you understand
that when you listen to my questions
and you don't laugh,
I think,
"What if Jesus is interested in me, too?"

Do you know
do you understand
that when I hear you talk about arguments
and conflict and scars from your past
that I think, "Maybe I *am* just a regular person
instead of a bad, no-good, little girl who deserves
    abuse."

If you care,
I think maybe He cares—
and then there's this flame of hope
that burns inside of me
and for a while
I am afraid to breathe
because it might go out.

Do you know
do you understand
that your words are His words?
Your face,
His face
to someone like me?

Please be who you say you are.
Please, God, don't let this be another trick.
Please let this be real.
Please.

Do you know
do you understand
that you represent
Jesus to me?

Sharon was surprised by the light she saw in others, and
she ended up taking a chance on God. She's in her late twenties and is another Buster who's had a tough time finding a job;
she works for a packaging company. Her dad left home when
she was very young. There was no male figure in her life, and

as she grew up, sex became her way of trying to feel loved and cared for. Because she felt that nobody cared. She was a true prodigal.

As an adult, she moved from one live-in boyfriend to another. She thought the pinnacle of life would be to be in the arms of a man, but she found the experience was shallow and hollow. She knew that sex wasn't meeting her needs at the core of her being. But she lived with guys because she deeply wanted somebody to take care of her.

Then she ran into Ruth, an old friend from high school, and reestablished that relationship. Ruth invited Sharon to Calvary Church. Because of her friend, and because she felt Calvary was relevant, Sharon kept coming back.

She joined a small group, and she got to know a group of people who had a unique outlook on life and who loved this person called Jesus Christ in a way she had never seen before. The friendships she formed there kept pointing the way to a relationship with a Father she had never known before. When the church was doing a series on emotions, she gave her life to Christ because she saw Jesus as a man who wouldn't let her down.

She wanted to break off her live-in arrangement because she knew it was a very destructive situation, and her relationship with her friends in the small group was pivotal to that. They helped her move out and even gave her a place to live rent-free until she could get back on her feet again. People rallied around her. It was real; it was rousing; it was relevant; it was relational. That's how God changes lives. That's a frequent occurrence among Buster ministries, as Sharon can attest.

When you're real, you gain Busters' trust. When you're rousing, you gain their attention. When you're relevant, you speak their language. And when you're relational, you build bridges to the next generation. To previous generations these were important ingredients in ministry. To the Buster generation, these ingredients are essential. Without them, you'll not engage the heart, mind, and soul of this new generation.

# Chapter 11

# Making the Connection: Reaching Busters

Bear one another's burdens.
—Galatians 6:2 (NKJV)

Randy just graduated from college and freely admits that he's been on a spiritual search for a couple of years. His friend, Carole, is a Christian and has been praying for him throughout that time.

"Randy has a bitter taste in his mouth about Christianity," Carole said. "He was interested in this girl named Lora, but she said she couldn't get involved with him because she was a Christian. That really rubbed him the wrong way."

But after a while, Carole noticed that Randy was asking a lot of questions and reading a few books about Christianity. He thought that if he became a Christian, he would have a shot at the girl of his dreams. Carole lost track of Randy for about a year; when she ran into him again, Lora was out of the picture, but Randy hadn't given up his search.

"I realized I was doing it for the wrong reasons," he told Carole. "If I want to find out about God, I have to do it for myself. I still think there are no absolutes, but I know there must be some higher power out there. I just don't want to call him Jesus."

That was a year ago. Ten months later, Carole and Randy had another deep conversation. Randy was shaken. "I'm tired of doing this," he said. "I know I said I don't want to be a Christian, and I'm still not ready to. But I need something to stand on. I can't be on shaky ground anymore. I really want to explore Christianity and figure these things out."

## AN UNREACHED PEOPLE IN OUR MIDST

What can we do to help a person like Randy understand that Jesus is relevant today?

In our ministries, we try to build alternative bridges to the Buster generation. We're not saying that traditional, mainline, or liturgical churches are unable to reach young people; some can and do. The fact that an album of Gregorian chants by Spanish monks took the pop charts by storm and sold more than a million copies in the U.S. shows that young people looking for inner peace find something quite moving about ancient traditions. But in our ministry, we simply offer some models for ministry that may be adapted by men and women who hope to create new churches for Busters or develop Buster services or outreaches within existing churches.

The paradigm shift that we've embraced and that we are encouraging people to consider is not meant to be threatening. If you're a pastor, for instance, you might be saying to yourself, "I'm just starting to consider what I might do to encourage Baby Boomers to consider Christianity. I don't know if I have the resources to revamp our programs for the next generation."

That's a valid concern, but bear this in mind: Subsequent generations, which are growing up in an environment in which the four forces (postmodernity, broken and blended families, the media, and the economy) outlined in part 2 are pervasive, will have much in common with the Busters. It is imperative that we begin to act now.

## IDENTIFICATION, NOT INSPIRATION

Churches that are trying to reach Baby Boomers take a different approach than what is needed to engage the thirty-and-under crowd. Boomers, as we have shown, simply have different values than Busters. In a Boomer service, the tone of the service and message tend to be, "Here's how to make life work."

If you look at the stage presentation of many contemporary-minded churches geared toward Baby Boomers, you'll find that it's one of *inspiration*. The atmosphere and staging is polished. The songs are sung beautifully, the dramas are professionally performed and the people onstage appear enthusiastic and bright. A Boomer service often presents an ideal: "You can become like this. These people's lives are a good example to follow."

But that doesn't usually work for Busters. They can't relate to such an ideal. Their attitude will either be one of despondency ("I can never hope to become like that") or detachment ("I don't know if I really want to be like that") or distrust ("I don't know if I can believe that"; or "this is too slick to be true").

What a Buster-oriented church would put onstage are young people who haven't arrived, whose lives are messy. That is attractive to other Busters, whose reaction is likely to be, "These people are just like me. They're going through the same stuff I'm going through." That is *identification*.

Busters aren't looking for answers as much as they are looking for people who can identify with their questions. They're not looking for success as much as they're looking for people who identify with their struggle. And that creates an environment of inclusiveness—they're not on the outside looking in. They're on the inside, even if they haven't come forward at an altar call, even if they're just beginning to process what Christians believe.

Biblically speaking, it's kind of like John and Peter. John seems like he would fit in with a Boomer culture. He was warm and loving, he was close to Jesus, and his life presents something of an ideal for us to aspire to. But Peter is like a Buster. His life was messy. He's rough around the edges. He's kind of raw. He's capable of great triumph—and great failure. A mere seven verses after he becomes the first disciple to plainly declare that Jesus is the Son of God (Matt. 16:16), Jesus rebukes him and says Satan is influencing him as he tries to steer Jesus away from what Jesus knows is his destiny of suffering.

Here's one more analogy from popular culture for what we mean by inspiration and identification and how it applies to different age groups.

We've already mentioned *The Real World*, the MTV program. MTV carefully selects a group of telegenic twentysomethings who usually have a fairly exotic array of occupations or aspirations—poets, musicians, actors. But once they've thrown these half-dozen strangers together in a house, it's not acting, it's not situation comedy. It's just a crew of video cameras taping these people's lives, and those lives are often tousled.

*The Real World* (and its travelogue companion, *Road Rules*) is a TV touchstone for Busters. It's not a contrived situation someone dreamed up like *Home Improvement* or *Seinfeld*. Look at *The Cosby Show*. What was Bill Cosby doing? He was stirring up Boomers, inspiring Boomers—"I want to be a dad like that." Now, look at *The Real World*. It's not inspiration, it's identification. To the Buster, life is all the drama they can handle.

When we utilize the reality of our lives to express our faith and make a point to Busters, we are following Jesus' model. Jesus was intent on identification. He showed the drama in real life. And Jesus' life was messy, too. He associated with prostitutes and tax collectors, who were some of the most vilified people in first-century Jewish society. Thus, our emphasis on identification is crucial.

Boomer churches have done a tremendous job of reaching the people of their generation. They create appealing and inspiring portraits of how fulfilling the Christian life can be through drama and other vehicles. But there is sometimes a gap, a moat, between audience and stage. To relate to Busters, we need to go one step beyond. We need to let Busters become the portrait. Busters want to get involved, and if we want to reach them, we need to build a bridge between the audience and the stage as well.

## POTLUCK PARTICIPATION

A Boomer service is like a five-course meal at a fine French restaurant. Each course is meticulously prepared, and then presented with panache by a polished server while the diner quite rightly basks in the high quality of the haute cuisine.

But Busters like a rawer reality in their service. It's like a potluck meal. Someone may bring a pasta salad, another may bring Chinese food, another may serve up some corn bread. None of it necessarily goes together, but the Busters usually don't mind. What matters is that they contributed; their role, however large or small, had value. And what was most important was the conversation, not the cuisine.

A Buster service is an environment where people are coming and not just listening; it's a place where people are coming and encountering.

They're encountering one another and where they're at in each other's lives; they're encountering how God is at work in people's lives; and they're encountering a message of hope as it is presented from the front and shared among each other.

How is this accomplished? Through stories. A Buster service is interactive. Suppose you raise a relevant question from the stage: "What do you think Jesus thinks of the welfare system?" Instead of a speaker answering that and elaborating on it for forty-five minutes, you could have brief break-out sessions where people turn to three or four people around them and discuss that topic for a few minutes. That breaks down some more walls—the walls between leader and audience and the walls between the Busters themselves.

Each group ideally would have both believers and seekers in them, and that is where the importance of training leaders or facilitators comes in, which we'll address in a later chapter. The questions are bantered about, and people have a chance to discuss them or perhaps even to ask more questions.

One distinctive that separates this situation from other church situations you may have encountered is that everything is not wrapped up neatly at the end. While a leader will address, in a short talk, what the Bible has to say about welfare, that message is merely offering a second helping of food for thought. Remember, life change most frequently will not occur among Busters in a church service or a large group setting. For the most part, Busters will only make a commitment to embrace Christ among their peers or a small-group setting.

Large-group meetings merely lay down the groundwork, lower the drawbridge, and tear down the walls so that life change can occur in more intimate settings.

With a postmodern mindset, Busters process truth relationally. In order for them to sort through an issue, or delve into the deep waters of their emotional makeup, they need time to process the radical message of Jesus. They need to think about it, talk about it among their friends, and talk about it some more. That process probably isn't going to be finished in an hour or two. Or maybe even a month or two. It may just begin during that time frame. When you try to wrap things up nice and tidy, Busters sometimes will see that as being unreal and trite; you minimize their search. We need to constantly remind ourselves that God doesn't need techniques to accomplish what his Holy Spirit sets out to do in someone's heart.

So just be real. Be vulnerable. It's a low-tech, high-touch approach to communication that conveys trust and value. It shows Busters that you sincerely value their input. And it shows the people who believe deeply in the mission of Christ and in the church that you trust them enough to put the responsibility for facilitating this life-on-life communication in their hands.

## GETTING IN TUNE

We have stated before that Busters don't want to be entertained; they want to be engaged. So when we use a medium that they're familiar with, excellence is quite important.

If "music is the kids' religion," as sociologist Donna Gaines puts it in *Teenage Wasteland*, we need to rise to the occasion when we use that medium to convey the meaning of God to Busters. The music we utilize must be relevant and real. The music can run the gamut in terms of style, but it's something that Busters relate to. The music expresses things that they're feeling. We want to use a medium they're familiar and comfortable with. We want to enable Busters to say, "This church identifies with me, in places of my pain, in issues of my experience. And the message and the music is being spoken and sung by people who are imperfect and in process, people who are human, people who are of my generation."

Music is much more important to Busters than it ever was to other generations. We're not afraid to use a song by Hootie and the Blowfish or a Counting Crows tune. It's important to validate their search, identify with where they're coming from, and that often ties in with what they're listening to. By using secular songs as a bridge into people's lives, we're not saying that we agree with every lyric or that we buy into the band's lifestyle—and we have strict biblical limits on the lyrics we'll use. We're simply communicating to Busters that we know where they're coming from. And as we showed earlier, Buster songs are full of searching.

Music is a powerful force, and it's an area that can be approached from a variety of angles.

When you're trying to make Jesus relevant to a person with no church background, some people believe that using a Christian song will provide very little identification and relevance for that person.

What Calvary Church is trying to say by using, for instance, an R.E.M. song is, "This song is part of your experience. It's already touched you. Now, let's take a look at what meaning we can derive from it in light of truth, God's truth." That's what relevance is all about. That's what being a missionary is all about—finding redemptive analogies in the culture in which he or she works. That's what Calvary is doing—redeeming the songs and using them for godly purposes. This sounds radical, but it's nothing new—the organ used to be a barroom instrument, and people like Martin Luther and Charles Wesley adapted tavern songs to convey Christian messages.

## THE COMMUNITY OF WORSHIP

Others in Buster ministry believe worship can be effective in ministering to the next generation; it's not something that should be shied away from if it's done right.

Worship, or praise, when done well, can serve as another medium for conveying truth in a relational manner. Why? Because it's not just one person proclaiming an idea through a sermon or a song or a drama, it's an entire group affirming a particular truth. And you're inviting your guests to be surrounded by that or even to participate in it by singing along.

At New Song, for instance, worship is very relevant music. The slogan is "Where the Flock Likes to Rock," and worship is put right up at the beginning of the service, because it can be engaging. No one is forced to participate. But the music is of a very high caliber. It creates an environment in which the church is saying, "We're Christians. We've received amazing grace from God. We continue to reach out and try to gain in the knowledge of who he is, and we look forward to sharing that joyful experience with you." Many of the songs describe characteristics of Jesus that have great meaning for Busters, like how God is a refuge for us. That's a great need among this generation, to have some place to go or someone to go to when we don't know where to turn. Some people simply stand and sing during the worship, some clap, some raise their hands during the songs, but everyone is accepted. The attitude is: "Wherever you're at, we accept you. We welcome you."

If you do it right, worship is not divisive, it's inclusive. It expresses community. It creates community.

People will often say that they find themselves singing the songs to themselves at work or at home during the week and that, when they thought about the words to the songs, they began to seriously consider how much they really needed God in their lives.

## THE BIG PICTURE

For the past decade, we have been working with Busters and trying to communicate the Gospel in a language they can understand. Sometimes we have succeeded; sometimes we have failed. But we are determined to make Christianity a viable alternative in the Athens-like atmosphere of contemporary American society. With that in mind, we add up our four R's in an equation, and the result is "interactive." As you absorb the new way of "doing church" that we describe, think about how this idea can be incorporated in your life if you're not a pastor. Think about how you can make your friendships, your work, and every other sphere of your life "interactive." But for a big picture, for a community-wide picture, try to picture a church service like this:

- A song, secular or Christian, engages the audience and creates a mood or raises a question. Let's say it's about a common Buster emotion: fear.
- A film clip from a recent movie looks at the lighter side of fear.
- A Buster gets onstage and introduces the topic, then asks, "What's the silliest or most irrational fear you've ever had? Turn to three or four people around you and talk about that for a couple of minutes."
- The stage and microphone is open for any who want to share their fears, or perhaps raise another question.

- A drama or skit explores fear, followed by a story or testimony from a Buster about how he or she has dealt with fear.
- A Buster or leader then shares what the Bible says about fear, and raises another question for group discussion and open-mike time: "If God could take one area of fear completely out of your life, what would it be?"
- When that has been talked out, a Buster or leader gives some direction or application to the issues that have been raised, and then a song ends the service. There is no strong sense of closure or finality—for anyone who cares to linger for awhile, the issues can be mulled at a post-service coffeehouse by the "instant" small groups that were formed during the interactive parts of the service.

One pastor who is developing a service for Busters within a Baby Boomer church talked about fear in a core group meeting very similar to the scenario described above. He confessed that one of his big fears was skydiving and asked how many people had the same fear. Lots of people raised their hands. He asked a series of questions that whittled the field down, until finally he asked, "How many people would be willing to face that fear with me by skydiving if the church would pick up the tab?" Only five people were left after that one. Through a random selection, a young woman named Kelly was chosen.

The next week, the two went up in the air. The pastor was frightened, and Kelly was crying. But after their feet touched the earth, Kelly was transformed. She was fired up; she had conquered a major fear in her life, and that promised to have far-reaching implications in other areas of fear in her life and her ministry to others around her. It was something she'll remember for the rest of her life. The next week, the core group watched a videotape of the jump, and those images would become a major memory for them as well. It was real, it was relevant, it was relational, it was rousing.

This is not a marketing-driven approach to church. It's simply recognizing the four major societal forces that have shaped Busters and trying to adapt your approach to conveying the Gospel. It's putting into practice the words of the apostle Paul in 1 Corinthians 9: "I have become all things to all men so that by all possible means I might save some." This approach— as evidenced by the skydiving scenario—is also a lot of fun. God gave us the free gift of eternal life; that is something to celebrate. In the pages that follow, we'll take a look at the elements that make ministering to Busters a difficult but dynamic endeavor.

# Chapter 12

# Hold My Hand:
# Teaching Busters

For God did not send his Son into the world to condemn the world, but to save the world through him.

—John 3:17

Everybody talks about John 3:16," said David, a twenty-year-old, "but a lot of people overlook John 3:17."

Condemnation is a concept that many Busters equate with God, and it's one that David has to battle every day. He's an entertainer, part of a performance troupe, and many of his coworkers are homosexuals in the Buster age group. David sometimes faces a lot of intimidation and disdain on the job, but he sees it as a challenge. He wants to prove to the gay men he knows that God and Christians are not breathing fire and brimstone.

"You get persecuted." He shrugs. "But love wins over everything."

David hosts a Bible study on his break at work, and a couple of his gay coworkers have become Christians as a result. Though many of the others are hostile when the staff is together, David finds a different spirit present in one-on-one settings.

"They put their boxing gloves down," he says. "They ask a lot of questions, and we have some great conversations. A lot of their questions revolve around whether God loves everybody."

There's no magic formula for David's success among his coworkers. He hasn't passed out pamphlets detailing a philosophical proof of the Gospel. He's merely practiced what he's preached; his faith has been *incarnational*. People have seen that David's brand of Christianity is attractive, relevant, and true.

## THE GOSPEL: ATTRACTIVE, RELEVANT, AND TRUE

Communicating truth to a postmodern mind can be difficult. If a group of people say they don't believe there's absolute truth, how do we begin to help them process the truth? Let us suggest what theologian Alister McGrath suggests.

The first thing we have to do is start with the attractiveness of what we're trying to communicate. We don't just start by saying, "This is true because it's true." We start by saying, "This is attractive. Wouldn't you like to take a closer look?" We seek to draw their attention to the attractiveness of the message.

The attractiveness of the message is very important—because the Christian message is very appealing. Two of the most attractive biblical concepts to the Buster, although they wouldn't think of it in these terms themselves, are *redemption* and *reconciliation*.

One way of looking at redemption, as a Buster pointed out to us, is recycling. Redemption is taking something that should be thrown away and making it useful again. And that's where Busters are at. They don't think they're usable. But the Gospel says, not only are they usable, they're valuable, and God wants to use them to affect others for eternity.

What's reconciliation? Making peace. Making peace with whom? Our heavenly Father and other people. What brings about so much anguish within Busters' lives? The lack of reconciliation—with their family and with their society. That is what the Gospel is all about, when it gets right down to it. It's about experiencing redemption and reconciliation at the initiative of our heavenly Father, who loves us and wants us to experience that so much that he gave up the most precious thing he had, his Son. And it is not exclusive, it's inclusive—he desires for the whole world to come to repentance and experience this.

When you begin to dig into the Scriptures and focus on those kinds of attractive issues, you find Busters draw a little bit closer. They'll say, "Well, I thought it was about staying out of hell." To which we respond, "Yes, it's about that, but it's more about love than staying out of hell."

Relevance is the second aspect of communicating truth to a postmodern mind. We want to express to Busters that, not only are these concepts attractive, but they're practical and pertinent: You can experience them and they will make a definite difference in your life.

Kerrie found this out when she became involved in a New Age cult. A girlfriend had urged Kerrie to look into this group, which grew out of a controversial and popular 1960s seminar.

The cult's immersion weekend alone was expensive and draining. Kerrie was subjected to carefully choreographed hours of ridicule by the seminar leaders, who sought to undo the major formative experiences of Kerrie's past and make her "a clean slate," as they put it.

It worked. By the second day, some initiates ("weak ones," said the group leaders) had dropped out. Kerrie proved her strength by moving forward. The group's philosophy ("You are powerful and can create your own reality") stuck with Kerrie. Soon, she was making two- and three-hour drives from her home to assist with the seminars. But she couldn't get Jesus out of her mind. She had some friends who were Christians who didn't fit her preconceptions of how a "religious" person should act. One of them, her friend Lauren, was particularly supportive.

Lauren was there whenever Kerrie needed her—and lately, that seemed to be pretty often.

As Kerrie advanced through the ranks of the organization, she eventually became a personal assistant for the cult leaders. She would take care of their itineraries when they came into town. One middle-aged leader had at one time been a pastor of a mainline denomination.

"Who is Jesus?" she asked him.

He laughed. "Jesus is whoever I want him to be," he said.

But the question nagged at her and burdened her. She couldn't get away from it, so she simply tried to escape it. One night, driving home from a seminar, despondent, she looked up an old boyfriend and sought solace in sex. But as she left his apartment and headed home later that night, the emptiness grew.

"He didn't care about me," she thought. "He was just using me. But I was using him, too, so it's okay."

At that moment, she heard God speaking to her heart. "No, it wasn't, Kerrie. It was sin. You can try to rationalize it or excuse it, but it's still sin."

She tried to shake off the effect of those words pounding at the innermost part of her being, but God's words came back a second time. It was late when she got home, but she had to talk to someone. She called Lauren and poured her heart out to her friend. She knew she needed to make a break from the cult but didn't know how.

"Why don't you check out New Song Church tomorrow?" Lauren suggested. "It might help. The people are very caring, and God is really alive there."

Surrounded by people in her age group, Kerrie sensed a warmth in that hour at New Song that she'd never experienced in the cult.

"I think I cried all the way through the service," she says. The vibrancy packed into the New Song service was attractive to her, and the relevance of the message hit home. "I felt like God was speaking directly to me," she says. The next day, she met with two staff members at New Song who prayed with her as she called upon Jesus to deliver her from the powers of darkness that had bound her.

When God stepped in on that freeway in California and convicted Kerrie of her sin, she knew who to turn to—Lauren, who had lived out the truth of the Gospel in a way that was relevant and true. Today, five years later, some of the cult members occasionally call Kerrie to try to lure her back into the fold. But it hasn't worked. Kerrie's turned the tables; God has used her to help two of her girlfriends leave the cult and become Christians as well.

Once you've established the attractiveness and relevance of the Gospel, you come to what Kerrie discovered: the truth of the Gospel. "Do you want to know why this is attractive? Do you want to know why it's relevant? Because it's true. Test it out for yourself."

## THIS IS MY STORY

Kerrie's experience is a powerful example of how God can and does intervene in our lives. And as Kerrie has told her story, God has used it many times to awaken nonbelieving hearts to the possibility of a spiritual reality that they could experience as well. Kerrie's story, like other life stories, rouses Busters because it comes at them from a direction they didn't expect with unblinking directness and sincerity. Herein lies one of the most effective ways to communicate the attractive, relevant truth of the Gospel—through the telling of stories.

Busters are storytellers and story listeners. They love watching *Oprah*. They love hearing people's stories. Coupland's *Life After God* book is a series of stories. And the more we can get back to storytelling as a form of Christian communication, the more effective we're going to become as we go back to being like Jesus, who told stories and asked questions. That was his primary form of communication.

He didn't explicate theology as much as he told stories and asked questions. And through all those stories, there was theology, there was a picture of who his Father was, and as he asked questions, he would awaken in his listeners a realization that their lives were devoid of meaning.

Generations prior to the Busters wanted answers and linear, logical forms of reasoning. They wanted messages that had several logical points that could be readily applied in life. Busters are looking for answers too. But they want the answers couched in the context of life. That's why they like the Gospels and the Old Testament stories more than the Epistles. The Gospels and the Old Testament stories teach things about God and life through example, and Busters need that example to follow.

In most, if not all, of the teaching we do, we help people see the working out of a particular biblical truth in the context of life—either using our lives as examples or calling people up to the front to share how this truth has affected their lives. Yet, even in sharing these stories, we are careful not to just relate tales of success. We have people talk about how sometimes their faith falters, how their commitments get broken, and how God doesn't always answer our prayers the way we want him to. Busters crave real-life drama. And they will not settle for easy answers in a slick package.

## FELLOWSHIP WITH A SMALL *F*

Traditionally, we think of conversion as the doorway into the fellowship. You trust Christ, and then you're "in." Then you experience community and fellowship and people praying for you, and you for them. But with Busters, we need to move that boundary line so fellowship is offered to people before they've figured out what to make of this person named Jesus and these people who are following him. We think this will be an important part of their process.

We're talking about fellowship with a small *f.* We're talking about the communal experience of people figuring out together how to follow God and connect with him regularly and be his men and women on this planet. We need to involve Busters in fellowship, where they can rub up against followers of Christ, where they can listen to what's going on and see how people are striving, or maybe not striving, to apply what they've learned about Jesus. We need to let them see how conflict is being dealt with in the church. They're going to be spectators for quite awhile, but pretty soon, as you invite them in, opportunities will arise. You can ask them, "What can we be praying about for you?" Or, "Why don't you pray? God is interested in what you have to say too." That kind of an experience is going to lead people toward becoming a part of the capital *F* fellowship of Christ.

As David's story demonstrated at the beginning of this chapter, it's important to avoid being judgmental. From a biblical standpoint, for instance, living together is wrong. But how can we expect somebody to act like a believer unless he or she is one? A lot of times, we expect people to take on the form of something that they're not. Our attitude should be, "We love you just as you are. Down the road, as you gain a certain amount of trust with us and begin to embrace what Jesus Christ is all about because of the Holy Spirit working in your life, you'll begin to lay aside some things that are important to you now, because they won't seem quite that important to you in the future. But you're not there yet."

The message is simple: If you're going to be accepting of people who are not personally declaring allegiance to Christ, you don't draw lines in the sand. They'll draw their own lines in the sand later.

Just look at Jesus and his relationship with the Pharisees, the so-called "religious" people of his day and age. The Pharisees were an example of the "either you're in or you're out" mentality. Look at Jesus' rebuke of the Pharisees. Jesus told them, "You set rules that you yourselves can't keep. You are trying to create an exclusive group in which you are the only members."

Then look at Jesus. He spent time with prostitutes and drunkards so much so that he himself got labeled that way by these exclusive club members. We don't see in the biblical texts that Jesus required these outcasts to clean up their act before he would be friends with them, and he's God incarnate. How much more should we fallible, imperfect humans have this attitude? If Christians are to be the representation of Jesus on earth, the task we are called to be engaged in is to be spending time with people whose lives are not all together and to continually invite them to forsake the things that are damaging them and walk in the light and in righteousness.

Dennis arrived on the scene at New Song in the post-Dieter era. He's a blue-collar guy, a mechanic who never gave God much thought. He'd had very little exposure to churches.

Though he was never one to partake in drugs or alcohol, Dennis grew uneasy when he saw himself becoming immersed in what he calls "a self-absorbed lifestyle." But a broken ankle curtailed his penchant for thrill seeking via rock climbing and other activities, and a couple chance encounters with committed Christians ("coincidences," he called them) shattered some of his stereotypes. So when a friend invited him to New Song, he was ready to give it a try.

As a budget-minded Buster who has his own business, Dennis was impressed that church was held in a school gym. He found that refreshing. But more importantly, he found the messages to be "pertinent" and the staff to be convincingly transparent. "You could tell they really believed."

After five months of observing to see if the people were authentic, Dennis was ready to take God at his word. Today, he volunteers in the Kids Konnection at New Song and calls it "the most fulfilled, most purposeful time I've ever known.

"If you had told me two years ago that I'd be getting up early on Sunday morning to study the Bible with the pastor and then go to church later on that morning and find ways to help first and second graders understand that God really cares about them, I'd have said you were nuts." Dennis's involvement in the fellowship of New Song led him to join the fellowship of Christ.

## "IN PROCESS"

Some of these concepts may not seem so new and revolutionary to you. But for the majority of the population, Christian community and the path to wholeness it offers is a foreign concept. We need to give Busters the freedom to process something that's very attractive but also very different from anything they've thought, seen, or heard before.

"Process" is a key word for Busters. They need time to process their thoughts and emotions when they see a genuine Christian community. David's friends didn't embrace Jesus instantly; Kerrie and Dennis looked long and hard at friends they knew they could trust before they were ready to trust Jesus with their lives.

Busters need to know that all of us are "in process." None of us have arrived. Sharing our stories with each other lets them know that even though we have embraced the free gift of grace through Jesus Christ, we're not perfect. We don't have it all together. We don't have all the answers. But we can share our joys and struggles with them as we articulate our journey of faith.

Where are these stories shared? Where is trust and community built? In most cases, the starting point is a small group, which we'll examine more closely in the next chapter.

# Chapter 13

# We Can Work It Out: Involving Busters

Taste and see that the Lord is good.

—Psalm 34:8

Shona was perplexed about which direction to go with her life as she graduated from college. Her friends were lassoing their diplomas around lower rungs in the corporate ladder, but her experiences as a Christian at a secular college had changed her ambitions despite her degree in business.

She saw clearly why some of her peers were fearful of testing the waters when it came to Jesus. "The hardest thing for them to accept," she says, "is surrendering control of your life to God."

Shona had crossed that bridge earlier in her collegiate years. She knew she wanted to work in a job that allowed her to interact with her peers. She was the leader of a small group for college students and didn't want to lose that sense of community and connectedness.

"After graduation, I went away on a silent retreat," she says. "I had chosen not to interview with any of the firms recruiting on campus because I didn't believe that was the direction God wanted me to go. But I really struggled."

She thought about her goals. What was it that she wanted? "Deep down, what I really wanted was to see my campus and other college campuses come to life and that people would have a desire to know Christ. I remember writing in my journal, 'I think what I really want is an administrative position at a college.'"

Shortly thereafter, she was talking with a friend on the phone who mentioned that Shona's college was searching feverishly for a recent graduate to fill a job in the development office. The post would entail working with students five nights a week. Shona was hired the next day.

It's not glamorous, and it doesn't pay nearly as much as her friends make in the "Microserf" world. But she's happy. She knows she's right where God wants her to be.

## SMALL GROUPS CHANGE LIVES

Like Shona, many Busters don't want acclaim, they want affirmation; and the small group is the most effective way for bringing about life change, for helping people experience affirmation while they are being conformed to the image of Jesus.

Small groups give Busters a chance to feel connected to their peers in an intimate relationship. It also fits in with their grass-roots orientation and being part of a team. Even for Busters who are still processing Christianity, involvement in a small group fills some of their relational needs in a real and relevant way. They may not believe in your God yet, but they really like being a part of something that they identify with.

Our small groups come in a variety of shapes and sizes. Most people find their place in a home group where ten or twelve people gather weekly to share what's going on in each others' lives, pray for each other, and perhaps study the Bible. Other groups form out of deep emotional needs, like recovery groups. And others may revolve around a shared interest or hobby. We've had small groups that were as simple as some people who enjoyed mountain biking. You're giving Busters permission to be a part of something they enjoy. You're enabling them to give and not just receive. That's very fulfilling.

A lot of ideas simply flow from people if you just ask them. Let's say you're talking to a young woman in your church. "Angela," you say, "what do you think you can do that will help us achieve some common ground with some people who are checking out the church and exploring what Christianity is all about?"

"Well," says Angela, "I'm kind of into rock climbing."

"Would you be interested in saying, 'Hey, a bunch of us are going rock climbing on Saturday; join us if you want'?"

"Sure, I could do that."

It doesn't have to be complicated. Maybe you and some friends from work or school are big football fans or big alternative-rock fans. Why not get together for a game or a concert and get to know each other better? Remember, relationships are the passkey to life change.

When Busters venture into the leadership of small groups, they often desire two things: guidance and autonomy. Since many Busters are still trying to take care of their own lives, they have little experience in shepherding other people. They need guidance and regular, personal support. On the other hand, they do not want someone telling them exactly what to do. They have their own ideas and passions and want to be trusted and believed in.

So how do you offer strong guidance and autonomy simultaneously? We organized all of our small group leaders under "coaches." Coaches are proven small group leaders who feel ready to lead leaders. These coaches meet every week or every other week with the leaders for prayer and support. Busters not only need this, they thrive on it.

This high touch/loose control approach to supporting our leaders has allowed many Busters to try out their leadership wings for the first time. It has also provided a very effective, enthusiastic set of groups that touched and changed many lives in the context of a vibrant, Christ-centered community.

## MEETING DEEPER NEEDS

It is perhaps a sad irony that one of most Busters' deepest longings—fulfilling relationships—is one they're ill-equipped to experience because of the twin forces of broken families and postmodernism.

This has spurred us to make far-reaching changes in the way we attempt to meet their needs. For instance, how would you talk to Busters about marriage? Many churches do indeed have premarital seminars. But the standard format for such activities is usually something like this: People walk into a room. They get a book. And then someone talks at them for an hour. If it's a six-session seminar, they'll probably get six hours of lecture. We have found that this format simply doesn't hold people's attention.

Calvary holds a lot of seminars, but there's not much lecturing. Tim and his wife hold a premarital seminar in their home that's very real and relevant. They share the story of their early years of marriage, which were quite rocky, but, like all of Calvary's seminars, it's a "chat-discuss," "chat-discuss" format.

Like the break-out sessions we mentioned in the last chapter, we want to get people involved by talking among themselves and making their own decisions. Other couples come in and share their stories before the group and older couples act as mentors for newlyweds during their first year of marriage.

Now, some people reading this book may say, "But we already have premarital counseling. We already have small groups." But are they set up in an interactive way that will make an impact with the next generation? Busters may need guidance, but they also want to give input. The chat-discuss format allows this to happen.

Small groups are often the means by which Busters can carefully consider the claims of Christ. The church needs to be a place of comfort and healing for Busters. At New Song, there's a vast array of support-type groups and recovery groups, from survivors of rape, to survivors of incest, to everything from AA to ACA to NA to SA—every type of "A" around!

At Calvary, recovery groups often spring up out of a one-day seminar called "Shame Off You" that is held periodically. Some Busters have heard "shame on you" all their lives—from their parents, from the media, from employers, from people who used and abused them. The seminar offers numerous break-out sessions, where people form small groups to discuss an issue. People sign up for the seminar looking for paths to healing, and "Shame Off You" tries to provide that. Besides the mental-health professional who runs the session, the group includes several people who have been through a previous seminar and now want to help others experience similar comfort.

In the break-out sessions, relationships begin to be formed and bridges are extended. Let's say, for instance, that a woman named Sue is a survivor of incest who has experienced some healing after going through a previous "Shame Off You" seminar. At a subsequent "Shame Off You," she'll be the leader of a break-out discussion session and simply say, "I'm going to be leading a recovery group at my house next Tuesday night for survivors of incest. Would you like to be a part of it?" As that recovery group forms and grows, relationships develop and hopefully some healing and comfort can be found.

In the area of counseling, it's very important for anyone who wants to minister to Busters to have a highly developed referral system so that people who are deeply broken can be channeled to a professional.

At New Song, a benevolence fund was established and it was recognized that a lot of the money in that account was going to go for short-term counseling. So the staff was able to say, "Here's a person we recommend that you go and see and, by the way, not only do we recommend that you go to see this person, but for 10 weeks, we'll support that financially." New Song would then partner with the counselor to help bring about healing and wholeness in that person.

## UNLOCKING THEIR IDENTITIES (GIFTS AND PASSIONS)

Motivation for involvement flows when a Buster begins to understand how and why God made them. We need to help them understand their identity on every level, including a theological one. Busters, like all of us who have trusted Jesus, are victors in Christ, but don't be surprised if you encounter some resistance to that concept. Busters will have a hard time believing that, because deep down they tend to be a guilt-ridden, shame-filled generation. They feel like losers. Even though they won't come right out and admit that, they wrestle constantly with it. They look so together, so cool and confident on the outside, but they're broken on the inside.

So when you try to help them understand that God loves them and he's purified them and their souls are whiter than snow now because the blood of Christ has cleansed them, they may nod their heads, but they'll have a hard time believing it. Give them time; remember, it's a patience game.

Besides affirming them on a theological level, let them know that God has wired them in unique ways. We believe that God gives people spiritual gifts. Some people are gifted in teaching and communication and others are great mercy givers. We involve Busters as we help them understand and discover the spiritual gifts God has given them. There are very few things more exciting to us than watching Busters who had become convinced that they were of little use to anyone, including God, explode in enthusiastic service after they realize that God has equipped them with gifts and that he wants to use them to change the world.

Besides gifts, we also help people identify their passions. People have passions for different things. Some people are very passionate about evangelism and others aren't. Others still need to be obedient to the work of evangelism, but perhaps they are passionate about coming alongside hurting people and taking care of them. When people discover their passions, they are better prepared to focus their gifts.

We teach about gifts and passions, and we also do some teaching about personalities. We use a personality test that lets people know if they are thinkers or feelers, introverts or extroverts, intuitive or sensory. And people find this fun and fulfilling because they begin to figure themselves out for the first time.

A feeler says, "Why don't you have a heart?" A thinker says, "Why don't you ever think?"

An extrovert loves to be in front of a group. An introvert loves people, too, but one at a time.

You can always tell an intuitive person by his or her little phrase, "Trust me." A sensory person says, "Why can't you ever get a plan?" To which the intuitive person replies, "Why can't you loosen up?"

They're all different. There's no greater spiritual value to one than the other. But we help people figure themselves out, and when we do, we find we really aid the cause of Christ— when people function as the individuals they've been created to be, they function in a self-motivated manner. You don't have to light a fire underneath them. They provide their own kindling, their own matches. And they will be forever grateful to you for helping unlock the mystery of themselves.

Every time Busters move into a ministry role, we sit down with them and develop a ministry job description that's personalized. We work with them and dialogue about what they want to accomplish. It's a relationship.

When you let Busters create ministries, you come up with all sorts of things that are meaningful to them, things that you might think won't work. At Phil's church, they have a thriving recycling ministry. At first, Phil was thinking, "This isn't all that important."

But Busters are very conscious of the environment. Recycling is good stewardship, a biblical value. One day, a group of Busters from the recycling ministry crashed the church office. They were going over it with a fine-tooth comb.

They looked at the trash cans and said, "What's all this paper in here?"

"It's garbage," Phil said.

"Nope," they replied.

So they trained Phil and the rest of the staff. After that, Phil was sworn to putting certain types of paper in one box, and other paper in a different box. The garbage cans were emptier, and the recycling crew felt valued.

The bottom line in such a scenario is that we give people permission to develop new ministry approaches, which is what involving people is all about. We're not going to tell people what to do; we're going to get their input and help them help us know what the future is going to look like. Who could better help us figure out how to reach Busters than Busters?

Unlocking their identities is communicating that everyone is valuable, everyone is unique, everyone has a contribution to make and, guess what, God did all of that for you. Our message is, "God made you to make a unique contribution, and we want to help you discover what that is and give you permission to express it." That's a powerful statement to a generation that is searching for its identity, that wants to do more than sit on the sidelines.

In practical terms, you do this by involving them. You need to express quite clearly that in unlocking their identities and letting them express their gifts, you're not trying to just get somebody to do a job for you. This process is driven by their abilities, their gifts, and their passion for a particular area of ministry.

We help them identify what makes them unique, and we make sure it's person-centered and not institution-centered. Let's say a Buster named Ed is interested in getting involved with a ministry at church. We would say to Ed, "This is what seems to make you unique. Here are three or four possibilities where your gifts could be released to make an impact. Try them out, and see if any of them suit you."

## PERMISSION TO FAIL

Getting Busters involved is a step-by-step progression. Once you've helped them identify their unique gifts, passions, and personality, you need to let them step out in faith and not only experience success but also the freedom to fail. Don't criticize their failures. Celebrate failure with Busters, celebrate their willingness to try. Then teach them; help them learn from their mistakes.

At our churches, we kid each other about the "faux pas of the month."

We often say to the Busters we work with that "if you're not failing once in a while, you're probably not trying hard enough." We learn more through failure than we do through success. As in other spheres, a Buster's motivation for getting involved may have less to do with the goal or the cause than simply the relationships engendered in working together with other people.

Busters fear failure more than almost anything, because failure reemphasizes how they already to a large degree feel about themselves. A lot of times, they won't step across the drawbridge and get involved because they're paralyzed by a fear of failure.

When Busters lend their hands to a project, you need to realize that you're going to get their minds and hearts as well. They will expect you to listen and respond to their input and ideas. Busters are willing to do a job, but they want to have a say in shaping that job as well.

This type of approach gives them ownership of an area of ministry. We need to be willing to put our egos aside and let this happen. What we are advocating here is a true priesthood of believers. A lot of churches give lip service to "unleashing the laity," but the follow-through often isn't there. Busters truly want to be in on the ground floor for bringing redemption and reconciliation to their generation, but their radar for phoniness will let them know if you really intend to let them get involved or whether you're just spouting a slogan.

## SHORT-TERM MISSIONS

There is perhaps no greater means to the hands-on involvement that we're talking about than missions work. Busters are the leaders and missionaries of tomorrow, and short-term missions is a means of involving Busters that has immense ramifications.

Short-term missions are life-changing experiences for people. To get out of our culture and to see God use them is a powerful experience for a Buster or anyone else. We really encourage it and put a lot of money behind it. Busters love to travel, so missions is a natural fit. We've helped send Busters to Romania, India, France, the Dominican Republic, Mexico, Switzerland, Africa, and on and on. But while missions have an impact on the people that Busters visit in a foreign culture, it probably has a greater impact on the travelers themselves: It's not the life you're changing where you're going, it's the life that's being changed as you go.

Missions can be a true partnership. The Busters can finance part of the trip themselves. We want to be able to say, "We really affirm what you're doing. But at the same time, we want you to have the full experience of this kind of a trip, namely that you also trust God to provide the resources, so you need to develop some of your own, because missions is about developing faith as well as compassion."

We love short-term missions. They stretch people, but they're also a lot of fun. People learn a lot about themselves. And what makes sending and engaging in short-term missions so important is that it's an experience that cannot be quickly or easily forgotten. Busters come back fired up about people who are on the front lines around the world. And they also see that the mission field isn't just some overseas culture but the diversity in their backyard as well.

In southern California, where Calvary and New Song are located, you might start by having Busters minister to the needy in the Orange County community of Santa Ana. From there, they may move on to L.A., from L.A. to Tijuana, from Tijuana to Ensenada, from Ensenada to Mexico proper, and beyond. What you're doing is constantly expanding their horizons. And when they participate in the outreach, you don't have to explain it to them. They understand the meaning of missions because they're in the midst of it.

We have found that Busters are much more open to this kind of ministry because of their desire to embrace other cultures and other backgrounds and values. We've found it very valuable to think of missions as no longer "out there." In most cities across the U.S. now, missions is "right here," all around us.

We have a responsibility to reach out and give back to our community. Shona, the young woman whose story was highlighted at the beginning of this chapter, is certainly community-minded, and her story is an example of redefining the American Dream into a more biblical context. Busters like Shona have much to teach us as we pass on to them the mantle of leadership, a subject that we'll address in the final chapter.

# Chapter 14

# Lead Me On: Leading Busters and Developing Buster Leaders

Everyone who cares for the soul needs a person who will care for his or her soul.

—Dietrich Bonhoeffer

Brian leads a Buster church. He identifies a lot with the Buster attitude, but when it comes to management style, he tends to be very performance-oriented, very Boomerish. He fixes his eyes on the goal, and sometimes he's hurt his relationships with people in that process.

On one occasion, he was at a staff meeting reviewing an event the church had staged. "I didn't think it had gone well at all, especially the artistic part of it," he says. Ironically, it was the first project for Belinda, the woman he had hired to handle the drama, video, and other artistic-oriented elements of the service.

It was also Belinda's first staff meeting. Brian wasn't like a bull in a china shop, he was like a bull in a china factory. He spent forty-five minutes blasting away at what he viewed as the event's shortcomings. "If I had to rate this," he concluded, "I'd give it a negative seven."

Belinda sat back in her chair. She was nervous, she was shaking. But she looked at Brian and said, "Wasn't there anything good in it?" She paused. "I know this is my first staff meeting, but couldn't we have started out looking at what was positive instead of what was negative?"

That hit Brian right between the eyes. But he had a decision to make. How was he going to react? Was he going to be defensive? Was he going to try to intimidate Belinda? Or was he going to value her and her comments?

"You're right," Brian finally said. "What you said is so true. I was wrong."

So now Brian starts out every meeting by looking at what was positive in what the staff did, what was valuable. "The other people on staff tease me about it now," Brian says. "It's kind of become a little joke on me. But I learned."

If you're leading Busters, you need to learn to be transparent, to admit when you're wrong. We haven't seen that too much in church leadership styles of previous years. But you have to get used to saying, "Look, I'm human. I screwed up." You have to be secure enough in yourself to say that. And when you're honest with Busters, your stature soars in their eyes. They value that kind of transparency and integrity.

## LEADING BUSTERS

The book *Twentysomething* was geared primarily to the business world, but it offers some keen insights into how we should relate to the next generation. Think of what the following quote can mean for ministry: "Your success at leading Busters will be determined by one skill above all others: your ability to be flexible. How adaptable you are to shifting conditions, how responsive you are to bend to the situation—these capabilities will be the keys to your success."[1]

How does this play out as we seek to nurture a Buster's spiritual development? We've adapted four "Twentysomething" implications for leading Busters in a spiritual context:

First of all, *I can only lead someone I know.*[2] This may sound obvious, but it's a key point we can sometimes miss. The stronger that this relationship is, the more fellowship and leadership is going to flow between that bridge. This point was emphasized in a note from a small group leader who wrote,

> You've asked me to tell you if there's anything you can do for me. Well, there is something you can do for me—you can get to know me. The thing I value most in life is to know people and to be known by people—especially people who are leading me.

In the early years of Rob's Buster church, he found people occasionally interested in helping him out with various projects he was engaged in at the time. "But they very quickly picked up on the fact that I was more interested in getting them to do something for me than I was in being there when the tables were turned, when they needed me," he says. "They were interested in relationship. I had to repent of that and let go of those expectations. I made a shift and made relationships with people my priority. I said, 'Let's just follow Christ together and see where that leads us.' As that began to happen and people began to sense a deepening of their relationship with me, we began to accomplish a great deal together."

A second implication for leading Busters is that *I am a coach*.[3] We'll explore this in detail later in this chapter but, for now, let's define what a coach is. A coach is not a supervisor. He is not someone who is there to check up on people; he is there to help people develop and excel according to the way they've been created.

Think of a coach on a high school basketball team. He's there to help you realize that you're a power forward, or a point guard, or a low-post center. He's there to put you in the right position, to help you learn that position, to help you succeed in that position. Why? So that you can become the best player you can be and maximize your contribution to the team.

- He observes.
- He lets you try.

- He gives constructive criticism.
- He cheers and challenges.

This list relates back to our discussion of gifts and passions. If you think of this in Christian terms, you would say, "I want to help you discover and become who God made you to be." That's an important part of creating credibility with a Buster. You're not trying to get them to do something for you, you're there to help them discover who God made them to be. You're there to fan that spark into a bonfire. That is very motivating to Busters.

Third, *I value people*.[4] We need to regularly communicate to Busters, "You're valuable to me." This must be communicated in very tangible ways. Ask what's going on in their lives—and then really, really listen. Take an interest in the full scope of their lives—not just the moments they're with you. And spend time with them. Everybody knows that time is valuable these days, and when you spend time with Busters, you demonstrate that they are valuable.

Fourth, *I involve people*.[5] That means we're regularly inviting them into decision-making structures, leadership opportunities, and very visible roles. If we borrow our coach metaphor again, it means we're continually pulling Busters into involvement and telling them that they can make an important contribution.

In a ministry built on small groups, this opens up many opportunities for Busters to step into leadership because we need a lot of people to lead those groups. Some of them, with a shaky self-esteem resulting from their family backgrounds, will tell us, "I can't be a leader." But we say, "We think you can, and we're here to help you do that. We're not going to abandon you." We put on our coach's hats again.

## MENTORING

Busters aren't looking for power as they get involved in leadership. For Busters, the payback is not taking the hill or accomplishing the project. The payback for being involved at a high level of commitment is that the Busters benefit relationally. They can play a part on a team, and they gain someone who's willing to mentor them, someone who is committed to them.

If Busters volunteer to get involved on a once-a-month basis in some capacity, they're not expecting much back in terms of time from leaders. But if they're willing to take a risk and step forward, for instance, as small-group leaders, they expect the people at the top to take a personal interest and make a personal commitment of time to interact with them.

When Dieter began to lay the groundwork for developing a Buster service at Willow Creek, it was apparent that one of the first things necessary was to develop a core group of young people who would be willing to lead small groups as people began reaching out to their peers who hadn't considered Christianity before. Since this took place at a large church like Willow, it was quite fortunate that seventy-five people stepped forward and expressed their willingness to be leaders. But their expectations of the leadership and the ministry that was unfolding were written all over their faces. They were saying, "We'll serve and lead in order to be around some of you who have a lot more experience in following Jesus than we do, and we expect you to give us some of your time and energy and spiritual direction."

Busters are looking for mentorship, something that their parents at times were unable or unwilling to give them. If you really want to see lives changed on a steady basis, if you don't want to see your efforts fizzle out after a quick start, you need to build the value of mentoring into the whole system and challenge people to mentor one another. As a coach, you need to develop other coaches. You find an experienced leader who's a little farther down the road and ask him or her to take on a small challenge: "Would you come alongside these three or four fledgling leaders and encourage them and give them some direction?" You try to empower the entire system. The traditional model of a pastor is that he's all things to all people.

With the relational and emotional needs of this new generation, we don't see how that can work anymore. Pastoring has got to be decentralized.

Think about how this would work with Allan, a member of your drama team. One person may help Allan with his acting, another may help him with spiritual matters, another may help him learn how to budget if that's a problem area for him. It may not even be intentional, but Busters are looking for opportunities to help each other.

## LEADING TOGETHER

Leadership is not done individually anymore, it's done together. This is difficult to swallow for any human being because of our own selfishness and propensity for individualism. We want to be seen, we want to be needed. But we need to share.

Recently, at a staff meeting at Calvary, Tim asked the other people on staff, "Where are you at? What's going on in your hearts in regard to how things are going here?" The reaction was swift, honest, and open.

John, a Buster who is the children's ministry leader, said, "I feel like we're all doing our own thing. My office is on one side of the building, Tim's office is over there, Ian's office is another place, Dan's office is over there—we're all kind of involved in our own little kingdoms but we're never intersecting or interacting."

He was right. So the leaders had to switch gears and make sure that in the future, they allowed time for togetherness in the midst of their work. But it goes beyond that. John wasn't merely saying that people weren't having a chance to interact with each other about the work that was being accomplished, he was saying that people weren't involved enough in each other's lives.

A Buster wants to be valued as a total person who has feelings and thoughts and hurts and needs that go beyond his or

her identity in the workplace. We need to say, "You are important to me as a person. Not your role. Not your job. You."
Even leaders' lives do not revolve around their role in leadership. They have interests outside of that role, and we need to
be involved with that part of them as well. "How's your family?
How's your volleyball team doing? I heard your mom has been
sick—how is she doing?" Be interested in the total person.
When you care about each other, you build community.

## DEVELOPING "WOUNDED HEALERS"

Busters carry a lot of pain with them, and they desperately
want to leave that baggage behind them on their journey.
They're looking for empathy. And once they've experienced
some freedom, they want to share that healing with each other.
That's why many of our small groups are set up with leaders
who are "wounded healers," a term coined by Henri Nouwen.
They're people who have been through the wringer and now
want to turn and offer their hand of support to others who are
struggling up the same cliff face.

Wounded healers reflect Paul's words in 2 Corinthians
1:3–4: "Praise be to the God and Father of our Lord Jesus
Christ, the Father of compassion and the God of all comfort,
who comforts us in all our troubles, so that we can comfort
those in any trouble with the comfort we ourselves have
received from God."

Wounded Busters need a lot of comfort. Not only do we
need to give Busters a lot of time to process the Gospel, but we
need to give them a lot of latitude to recover from their wounds.

Busters believe that you don't go someplace to "get
fixed." Healing your wounds is not a one-time deal or a ten-
time deal; it's a process. But they want to become whole. That
is a real longing among this generation. They want the broken parts of their life to be healed and they want their whole
life to make some sense. Their attitude is: "I don't want to
have this limp; I don't want to have this depression; I don't

want to have this gap; I don't want to have this dent in my life. I want my life to work."

The Christian life has to give them hope. One way for Busters to receive that hope is for them to interact with people who have been through what they're going through, or who are still going through the same thing but are further along in the healing process. They may be hurting, but they still want to be accepted. They want to be embraced. They want to hear people say to them, "It's okay for you to be that way. I'm not going to push away from you even when you're broken."

Buster leaders sometimes think, "I have to be this big, authoritative Bible study leader. I don't know if I can do it." But leaders are always told, "We just want you to facilitate the group. God has done something in your life. And whatever he's done, he can use that healing process to encourage someone else. So don't be afraid to say, 'Here's what happened in my life,' because there's a good chance a handful of people in your group are going to relate and grow from that."

## ON-RAMPS AND EXITS

When you're developing Busters as leaders, it's important to build flexibility into your system. There's got to be room for people to step into and out of leadership, and there's got to be room for people to move around within leadership as well. A lot of these leaders will be young and don't really know themselves that well yet.

When a person gets involved in leadership with us, we'll sit down with them after a couple months and ask them, "How's it going? How are you liking this? Do you feel like this is a good place for you, or do you feel like there's another place you'd like to try ministering in?"

Jon and Wendy are a very sharp couple, but they avoided getting involved in church leadership for the longest time. We didn't pressure them. What was interesting was that they often talked about getting involved, but they always held back. Then one day they sat down and said, "We're ready. We'd like to get involved in leadership. Where can we serve?"

It was an abrupt change. "What was it that changed your mind?" we asked.

"Well," said Jon, "you were talking about leadership in the service this past weekend. You talked about flexibility, and how we needed to treat each other as humans first and then as leaders. And I realized that the thing that has caused me not to want to get involved was the thought that I was signing my life away. But what you communicated to me over the weekend was that you would consider my feelings if I came to you and said, 'I can't lead' if things didn't work out. You wouldn't shame me and you wouldn't hold it against me."

That kind of flexibility, those on-ramps and exits, are what cause Busters to take little steps into leadership. Traditional rigidity won't work with them because they're scared of getting locked into something that they're not going to be able to get out of. This is another area where you have to be patient with them and understand that developing leaders can be something of a reparenting process because a lot of them don't have the life skills and relational skills people learn in a family.

## BUILDING BIGGER PEOPLE

We need to keep in check our human tendency to say, "We need more people to get this accomplished." Where we turned the corner in our ministries was when we said, "We want to build bigger people. We believe that in building bigger people, we're going to build the ministry."

Building bigger people may or may not build a bigger church. But at least when it's all said and done, you've accomplished something of value for the kingdom of God, and people's own value of themselves has gone up in the process.

Busters aren't looking for bells and whistles; they're just looking for permission to lead. Let's trace this through the typical Buster leadership role: the leader of the small group. How does a Buster lead a small group? We use a variation on the Carl George small-group model, which was Love, Learn, Do, and Decide. We say, "If you want to call yourself a small group, you've got to do four things: *love, learn, serve,* and *reach.*"

Now, every small group is going to look a little different. Some will be high in *love,* a little bit of *learn,* a little *serve,* a little *reach.* Others will be high in *serve,* but still have the other three elements. Some will be primarily involved in *reaching* out to people.

We divide the year into three trimesters—a trimester is long enough to give Busters freedom to chart their own course, but short enough for us to provide the mentoring they need. At the beginning of every trimester, we have each small-group leader fill out a projection sheet and tell us what they expect their group to look like. For instance, the leader of a rock climbing group might say, "Our group will be high in *love,* and have lots of *reach.*" To which we can respond, "Terrific. But what are you going to do in terms of *serving* and *learning*?" And they would have to tell us. You can do some serving for the church when you're not rock climbing, and there are all sorts of spiritual principles you can teach and learn using rock climbing as an example.

Someone else might say, "Our group is going to be an intense Bible study. It's going to be two-thirds *learning.*" To which we would say, "Fine. But you also have to tell us how you're going to help the people in your group grow in *love, serve,* and *reach.*" So we allow flexibility. They can define what they are going to do, but it has to be within certain parameters, and they basically have to make a case to us for why they are doing what they're doing.

And at the end of every trimester, we get together with them and have them fill out an evaluation sheet: "Look back over these last three months and tell us, what did it look like?" You're coming around again, following up, and getting a chance to say, "Great job" or "Here's an idea of how we can improve next time."

The four elements—*love*, *learn*, *serve*, and *reach*—give us focus and direction. But it also gives Busters boundaries, which they need, and flexibility and decision-making power, which they want. It provides them with high touch when you sit down with them at the beginning and end of each trimester, but it also gives you a chance to mentor them along the way.

Suppose a small-group leader says to us, "We're going to go through the book of Philippians this trimester. We're going to learn a lot. We're going to regularly spend time praying for each other (love), we're going to go down to the city and feed the homeless (serve), and we're going to regularly spend time each week praying for our friends and family who don't know Jesus (reach)."

Then, on a weekly basis, they give us a call and let us know how it's going. In such a dialogue, we're helping the leader follow through on the plan he or she designed. That puts us in a position of support, not authority.

It's rare that we as pastors ever have to pull the plug on a group that's not jelling. Usually, the leader will figure it out and come to us and say, "Hey, you know what? This just isn't me. It's not really working out." Maybe some other type of group will be a better fit for that person. You need to be flexible. We try to set our leaders up to win rather than to fail.

## TEAM: PUTTING IT ALL TOGETHER

Once you develop your infrastructure of leaders, how do you keep them motivated? How do you keep them unified? We found that we regularly need to devote a time of ministry specifically to these lay leaders. At Calvary, it's called Team Community. At New Song, Leadership Community is a variation on the same theme.

The purpose of a "team night" is simple: build up and bind together the core group of leaders. It's a time for the pastor to communicate the vision of the church to the people who are carrying out that vision. Sometimes it's a time for extensive praise, prayer, and worship. Other times, it's an evening for games and laughter and recognizing unsung heroes.

Community is our goal, and it's also what Busters are restlessly searching for. Let's look then at the components that make up community, the components that make up a high-performance team.

*Powerful purpose.* If you read any of the business literature that's coming out today, you'll find that the concept of "visionary leadership" keeps coming up again and again. For a team, powerful purpose means having a vision. Our vision for the church is to have people who have been saying no to God turn around and say yes. That is a purpose that is much bigger than ourselves, and a purpose people can rally behind.

*Empowering environment.* We need to communicate to people that they are important, that they have a contribution to make, and that they have the authority to act on different issues.

For example, let's look at a church preschool ministry. In most cases, the preschool leader is not paid. But in our church, the preschool leader is the one who sets the budget. When we have a decision that needs to be made on, say, the size of facility needed for the preschool, it's not the pastor or the board who comes in and simply states, "Here's what you need." We will go to that preschool director and ask her, "You're the person who is closest to this situation. What do you and your team need? Could you come to us with some idea or proposal? You're the experts on this."

In ninety-nine percent of the cases, we're going to approve that proposal. We totally empower the team. We want our team members to be impact players who feel an ownership in their area of ministry.

*Real relationships.* This is a crucial aspect because, in addition to the ministry teams needed to run any church, we have leaders who are part of a bigger team called small-group ministry.

Relationships contribute to the longevity of a person's interest in maintaining a continuing status on that team. We teach our leaders to create an environment where relationships are forged. People want to experience real community as part of their service, and if that need is being met, they will continue to serve and ministries will thrive. Without real community, ministry won't work. So often a ministry team, or a task team, will burn out if the team doesn't support and nurture each other.

It seems as if our society is becoming more and more dysfunctional, so to take it for granted that people know how to relate with each other is taking an unwarranted, giant leap.

*Fun and flexibility.* We want people to enjoy what they do. If they don't, we want them to get out of it, because they're not going to want to show up and do it.

We tell people that our ultimate goal is to create HIP people. HIP stands for High Impact Players. How do we do that? By making our local Christian community a fun place to be.

Sometimes it's as simple as a team or a small group going out together to a hockey game or a movie. We also have a Team Community night, where people come together to have fun and encourage each other. If everybody can laugh together, can let their hair down and act a little different, a lot of acceptance is created. When we get doctors and lawyers taking part in a water balloon toss with blue-collar workers, the walls come down. People start thinking, "Hey, this is a cool place to be."

*Optimal output.* We have to include this element because we do need to get a job done. Thus, we need excellence in the way a job is performed. We work a lot with our leaders in what's called a huddle time. As we mentioned in the previous chapter, we expect written goals and progress reports from our leaders and this is a key part in holding them accountable, which increases their effectiveness.

There's always a concern that you can expect too much from volunteers. But volunteers with a vision who are being cared for in an empowering environment and who are engaged in real relationships will indeed perform with optimal output. Everybody wants to succeed. Nobody wants to do a shoddy job. Everyone aspires to excellence. But when people aspire together as a team, they're asking, "What is the next level, and how can we get there and bring glory to God?"

*Rousing recognition.* Some people think that servanthood should be done in secret and thus it should not be recognized. We disagree. People need to be recognized. It's what drives us as human beings. In a volunteer organization, which is what every church is, the people who are part of that organization need to be recognized.

We have fun on the recognition scale. We give out awards. They don't cost much, but they mean the world to the people who get them. Sometimes they're zany, but people need to know that they will be caught doing something right.

One is the Giant Killer Award, which is engraved and has a slingshot on it. It goes to a volunteer who wants to become a leader and wants to tackle something brand new.

Another is the "You Can't Make It Tough Enough for Me to Want to Quit" award. This is a plaque with a piece of beef jerky on it, which goes to someone who is often overlooked but has hung in there. We present it as we play the theme music from the movie *Rocky*.

Another is the Lifesaver award, which is a plaque with a roll of Lifesavers candy on it, which goes to someone who has gone above and beyond the call of duty.

One time, one of our small-group coordinators got both the beef jerky and the Lifesaver awards. The person who coordinates small groups is often behind the scenes and doesn't get a lot of recognition. He's not out front preaching or playing guitar. But his skills are perhaps more important than a sermon or a song in putting people together in an environment in which they can connect with each other. When we surprised the small-group leader with the awards, he got a standing ovation. And he was crying. It turned out he had had a really rough week. He was disheartened and had prayed, "Lord, I'm really down. I don't feel like what I do is important. Please, please show me if what I'm doing is worthwhile and is pleasing to you." God was able to use us to powerfully communicate his love and acceptance to this man.

*Motivating morale.* We need to create an environment where people feel confident about their ministry, where people feel good about contributing.

If you've ever been part of an organization where morale is high, you know that it's the engine that drives the whole thing. It's the back end; the vision has to be the front end. When morale is high, there's a sense of team spirit. People's confidence and competence levels go up, and there's a cohesion that's created. That in turn creates a higher level of morale.

## WHAT LEADERSHIP LEADS TO

A natural outgrowth of Busters becoming leaders is church planting. If you are committed to leadership development, it will happen that some people that God has gifted and called are going to rise up and say, "We can't just do this here. We've got to have an example of Christian community in other places too." They've received on-the-job training; it's not just a classroom experience.

When Dieter left New Song to start a Buster ministry at Willow Creek, he did so with some trepidation. Busters struggle a lot with abandonment issues, so what happens when the founding pastor of a Buster church leaves? Does the whole thing collapse?

Far from it. New Song is thriving. The church is growing, groups are multiplying, ministries are expanding. They've planted another New Song church and soon will plant a third one. Instead of one person overseeing everything, an executive committee of four people functions as the senior management in different roles. New Song is doing wonderfully.

And so, that answers a question that may be in the back of your mind—can Busters really minister? It's one thing to reach out to them and bring them into the church. It's quite another to entrust an entire ministry to them and watch them succeed beyond description.

## WHAT ABOUT YOU?

When Busters come to church these days, they're asking a simple question: Do you want me here?

What will your answer be?

You have to start with your own convictions: "Do I want to reach this age group with the message of Jesus?" It's a big decision, because Busters are a messy group. You have to fight harder for credibility, you have to love harder to overcome their pasts, you have to accept the fact that it will probably take Busters a longer time to process the Gospel and risk surrendering their lives to Jesus.

But it starts with asking yourself the question, "Is this generation valuable to me, and can it be valuable to our church?" On an intellectual level, we would say "yes" instantly. Jesus came to seek and save the lost, and these wayward sons and daughters seem in desperate need of a reunion with their Father. But what about on an emotional level? Will you accept Busters? Will you value them? Will you reach out to them?

If you're a church planter, we hope you'll consider gearing some of your efforts specifically to this next generation. If you're a pastor, perhaps you can consider developing a service on an alternative day or evening specifically for Busters. If that's not possible, perhaps you could experiment with turning over one service a month or every two months to the Busters in your congregation. If you're not currently involved in church leadership, consider how you can encourage your pastor to value the next generation.

We hope that by taking some of the mystery out of Generation X and explaining some of the ways we've ministered to the Busters, we've encouraged you to consider taking just such a step. It's our hope and prayer that our churches will be imbued with community and will be places of refuge where Busters can see John 13:34 lived out daily: "By this all men will know that you are my disciples, if you love one another."

# Appendix 1

# The Story of New Song

**Dieter Zander**

In the early 1980s, I'd come down from Portland, Oregon, to go to seminary in Southern California. Part of my ministry assignment back then was to help coach soccer at a college in the area. I was attending a very vibrant, contemporary-minded church at the time called Community Baptist Church in Alta Loma. I was very excited about it and was encouraging some of the soccer players to come with me to church.

After much cajoling, a number of the players agreed to accompany me over the course of the season, but they never made a repeat visit. Finally, at the end of the season, I asked them one by one why they didn't want to go to church. They were very honest with me, and their answers fitted into three basic categories:

1. "Church is boring." They weren't saying it was boring for the people who went there; they believed that the people who attended church got a lot out of it. But for them personally, it didn't engage them. "It just doesn't fire me up," they'd say.
2. "Church is irrelevant." Again, they were sure that other people found it relevant, but church simply didn't connect with the issues they were encountering in their daily lives.

3. "There's no one like me at church." They saw church as a fine place for older people and for families raising their children, but they didn't see anyone in their age group at church.

Hearing those reasons again and again really affected me, because I saw that, through their eyes, they were right. Community Baptist was and is a wonderful church for Baby Boomers, but my soccer friends felt left out. It was with this in mind that my wife and I began to consider starting a church for a group we called "the people in between"—too young for mainstream church and too old for youth groups. These deliberations came to a head with an incident that occurred in 1984.

I was driving home from soccer practice and had just stopped at a stop sign when God gave me a brief vision. Now, visions are just not part of my experience. But I can't deny what happened. In a moment's time, this is what I saw: I was standing in the back of an auditorium looking up toward a stage. On the stage was a rock band and a drama group. There was theatrical lighting hovering above the stage, and I saw myself on that platform.

A couple days later, I was meeting with Bob Logan, the pastor of Community Baptist and my mentor.

"Bob," I said, "I have this idea. What about starting a church for young people?"

"Describe what you mean," he said.

I thought he'd laugh at me, but I described to him the scene I saw in the vision—though I didn't tell him it was a vision. After I had finished, he looked at me and said, "Our staff has been praying for two years for God to bring us someone to do exactly what you've described, and you're it. You're the answer to our prayers."

It was at that point that I told him that this was related to me in a vision, but he didn't bat an eye.

"You've got to start this church," he said.

That's how New Song was born. But I had a rough lesson to learn in the early going. I took God's vision and modified it.

I decided to try to reach not just people in their twenties, but punk rockers in their twenties. Between seminary and our first year of marriage and work, it took awhile to get New Song off the ground, but we went public in June 1986 with forty-two people, almost all of whom were punk rockers.

God let us try to do that for about two months. But then I discovered that one of the twentysomething punk rockers in leadership was sleeping with two of the women in the church. I called him on the carpet, and said, "Hey, you can't do this. This is wrong. This is sin."

And he said, "Who are you to tell me what to do?"

He spread a message throughout the forty-two people that I was being authoritarian and dictatorial, though he never acknowledged what our conflict was about. As a result, most of the people left New Song immediately.

At that point, I was immature in faith and immature in life. I took what was happening very personally—I would wake up in the middle of the night in cold sweats worrying about the future. So my wife and I paid a visit to Bob Logan. We sat across from him in his house and explained to him what had happened.

"Bob," I said, "I can't do this anymore. I don't want to do this."

"Dieter," he said, "What you're experiencing is called spiritual warfare. Satan doesn't want this church to work. Don't quit. I'm not going to let you quit."

So I didn't quit. Around the beginning of September, a whole new group of people started showing up to New Song services, people who'd heard about New Song through word of mouth. They weren't punk rockers. They were normal, straight-laced young people like my wife and me. Those fifteen or twenty people became the core for the restart of New Song.

We took our name from Psalm 40:3: "He put a new song in my mouth, a hymn of praise to our God. Many will see and fear and put their trust in the Lord." When the Bible talks about a new song, it's usually talking about a new work of God. That was what we believed God called us to.

In the beginning, we were pretty ragtag, but the vision and the format were there. We would sing some rock 'n' roll praise songs for twenty or twenty-five minutes, then welcome everyone and share the announcements. We might incorporate some drama and then I would give a message. Our vision was simple: "We are here to create a church for you and with you. We want to give you permission to create this ministry."

But the church didn't take off until I took the burden of creating the church off my shoulders and yielded it to God. When I would awaken at night, I would get up and go out in my living room and remember Jesus' words to Peter in Matthew 16:18: "On this rock I will build my church." And so, every night, I would pray, "Jesus, build your church. Just show me what part you want me to play in it." I prayed that every day until I left New Song. Looking back, I can see quite clearly the ebb and flow of our ministry:

1986–1988: I was finishing up seminary, and we were trying to find our identity as New Song. We were trying to answer the questions "What are we here for?" and "Do we really want to reach a generation where ministry may be limited because of meager financial resources?" We were growing up as a church, and attendance was about 100 to 120.

1989: A major breakthrough. It felt as if God said, "It's time. You're ready." We had a strong sense of God's guidance, strength, and energy, and we grew from 120 to 400. We faced crises with a gift of grace under pressure. We were meeting in the activities center of a local college. When the president discovered that a church was renting the facility, he ordered us out by the end of the year. With three weeks until the deadline, we had been unable to find a new home. Then, at the last minute, God provided us with a one-year lease at another local college, a bigger space at one-fourth the rent we had been paying.

1990: With the facility problem resolved in a stunning way, we felt like we were in the center of God's will. Our membership grew from 400 to more than 1,000 people with an average age of twenty-six. Almost all of them were single. Over the summer, I took my first study break, a three-week retreat from ministry. During this time, I realized that, despite our successes, we were primarily reaching dissatisfied churchgoers, not people who had little or no exposure to Christianity. This grieved me.

1991: Echoing Bill Hybels' words that "lost people matter to God," we began an occasional series of weekend services specifically targeted to seekers. It was also a year for building some much needed infrastructure. Though we had 1,000 people, we began the year with only twelve small groups. During this time, I realized that Busters' lives are more apt to change in small groups—not big weekend services—and we increased the number of our small groups to thirty and began Leadership Community as a means of empowering and inspiring our small-group leaders.

1992: On a summer night in 1992, I walked into the gym where we were setting up the stage for a New Song service and stopped dead in my tracks—the scene I saw was identical to the one in my vision eight years earlier. I felt like God was saying, "Well done. You've done what I wanted you to do." I also began to wonder if my mission at New Song might be drawing to a close. The end of the year was a dark time for New Song. We decided we needed to become like Willow Creek and attract seekers every week. We cut way back on worship, which had been New Song's identity. It didn't work. It wasn't who God called us to be, and people started leaving.

1993: We determined to start 1993 with a new, yet old, focus. We said, "Let's do New Song the way God intended for us to be." We put the worship back in and stopped trying to be something we weren't. And yet more people became Christians during these first few weeks than in all those dark months of '92 put together. It was a huge turning point. Yet I wasn't sure where to go from there. During my study break each year, I usually came back energized with a clear sense of where God was leading us. Yet after my study break of 1993, I didn't have a clue. When Willow Creek approached me in October, I began to explore if this might be the time to pass on the vision for New Song to the next generation.

1994: At the end of January, we made the decision to leave. We had a great send-off in March and, in our absence, the Busters on staff have demonstrated convincingly that they can be leaders. The church is stronger now than it was when I left. God wanted to show me that New Song's success was not based on my abilities, but on his power to build his church with, and through, Builders, Boomers, Busters, and beyond.

# Appendix 2

# The Story of Calvary Church Newport Mesa

## Tim Celek

Ten years ago, I was an assistant pastor at a megachurch in Southern California. I had joined the staff after a knee injury ended my wrestling career with Athletes in Action, the Campus Crusade outreach.

Back then, there were no books out on Busters. Baby Boomers dominated the media. I was overseeing the singles ministry and noticed that we didn't have any programs for the twentysomething crowd, an age group with whom I identified. So we started a program called 20-Plus, and it really took off. This aroused in me a desire to plant a church with some of the ideas I was developing in 20-Plus.

When my church gave me permission to start a church in 1988, I did some demographic research about the area I was going into. I found that there were two major colleges, a third smaller college, and a community college nearby. There were also many apartment buildings and condos in the area. Yet for the first year we tried to be all things to all people, and it didn't work.

As the year progressed, we realized we had to refine what we were doing. Who were we trying to reach? Who were the people who made up the majority of the physical community around us? Young people. Busters with very little exposure to any kind of Christianity.

If New Song is seeker sensitive, we're seeker targeted. We have to be if we want to reach the people who live in the community in which our church is located. We are very evangelism-oriented in our service; we speak their language and find redemptive analogies in contemporary culture to uncompromisingly communicate the saving grace of Jesus.

But in the early years, I tried to do it all myself. It just wasn't working, and I was ready to give up.

In the summer of 1990, I was sitting around talking with Ian, my associate pastor. I looked at him and said, "You know, if I have to do this for another fifteen years, where I have to work eighty hours a week and never see my family, where I have to meet with all these people all the time and try to motivate them, I'll never make it. I'm hardly making it as it is."

I realized that anyone who starts a business or a company or a church has to put in a lot of time in the early going to get the venture off the ground. But I saw no letup in sight. It was a hard time all around—even financially. I had taken a pay cut to start the church so the money that was coming in could be used to keep the church running. And there was no light at the end of the tunnel.

"This just isn't working," I told Ian.

I felt like I had failed Ian as well. I had recruited him to come on staff out of our previous church. He was incredibly loyal and he was an ex-athlete like me; we had a lot in common.

As we sat there—I don't know what prompted me to say this—I said, "Ian, let's talk about something happy. What was the greatest athletic feat that you ever accomplished?"

So we discussed our sports memories for awhile, and then switched gears a little bit. "What was the best team you were ever on," I asked him, "and what did it feel like?"

We talked about some of those teams, and then Ian posed the same question to me.

"When I was in high school, I was part of a really lousy football team in my freshman and sophomore years," I said. "Then, all of a sudden, this coach came in and he took players who were the same as the year before and turned us into winners. He took a team that was 2–8 the year before and helped us to become 8–2. We won the league!

"I'll tell you, Ian, I'll never forget banging on the lockers and whooping and hollering and screaming as we were winning games. There was no feeling that compared to the sense of camaraderie that I got from the rest of the guys on the team. That whole sense of enthusiasm and excitement—it was incredible. And I don't feel that at all right now. I want to feel that as a pastor."

As I told this to Ian, I found myself getting choked up. The tears started running down my face.

He looked at me and said, "Why are you crying?"

"Because I feel really isolated right now," I said. "I don't feel like I'm part of a team, and I don't feel like any of the people who are part of our core group feel like they're part of a team. All we're doing is putting on a show every weekend, putting on a program. But if we stop the program, I'm not really sure if anybody would really care. They might care at that immediate moment, but I'm not really sure they'd care a couple months down the road.

"Ian, I haven't been a part of a real team since that football team back in high school. And I would sure like a church to be like that, because I really think that's what Christianity is all about."

We started brainstorming, and Ian suggested that I share how I felt about our position with our core group of leaders, the people who helped make the church and services run. That year, we started something called Team Community, which you read about in the last chapter of the book.

We decided it was possible to make team happen, to create a winning team atmosphere. But it meant I had to stop trying to do everything. I had to be the coach and only the coach. I had to decide that I couldn't collect the tickets anymore. I couldn't be the cheerleader. I couldn't be the P.A. announcer. I couldn't be the quarterback and the person hiking the ball and the person going out for the pass. And when I made the decision to be the coach, it was a major switch, because it meant I was going to elevate players who were going to be more visible than I was as the coach.

Good coaches produce great players and championship teams by creating an atmosphere where unity exists. They're not doing it all. The players are going for the championship. Everyone understands their role and they carry that role out.

Implementing this decision to be a coach meant I had to get up and tell people that I couldn't do everything anymore. That was hard.

"My kids haven't seen me much," I told the people in our church. "My wife and I have a good relationship, but her tolerance is wearing thin. And I'm doing you a disservice because, by my attempts to do it all, I'm telling you that you're not valuable, that you don't have something to contribute.

"I'm going to believe God for the next five years," I said. "I'm going to believe that God has placed certain gifts in this church, and I'm going to let you utilize those gifts. All I'm going to do is prepare you. I will help you be focused, I will encourage you, and I will develop you to a high degree of competency so you can take pride in your performance or your work or your ministry."

That's what a coach does. And that was the turning point for me and for Calvary Church Newport Mesa. It was a change from a clergy-directed ministry to one where the focus was on developing leaders so they would do the ministry.

First Corinthians 12 talks about team as it applies to the body of Christ and how we are to unleash that. Ephesians 4 discusses how each part of the body does its own work and how this helps the body grow strong. It's God's way of saying that he wants to create a championship team.

This involves a different mindset. As we said earlier, it's one thing to talk about lay ministry and getting the laity involved, but it's another to actually do it. There's a fear factor involved, because people in charge—like me—often are reluctant to part with any of their decision-making powers.

As soon as you decide that you're going to be a coach, and that the players are more important, it's as if you've stepped out of an airplane with a parachute you're not quite sure about. You really have to rely on the people around you to carry out the mission of the church. You provide the game plan, but you have to rely on others to carry out that game plan.

I found out that there were a lot of people who did things better than I did. I thought people needed me to do it all. And I found out that was such a fallacy. What they needed was a framework where they could receive care and then carry out the ministries that God had equipped them to do.

Sometimes, we've tried to do too much too soon. In the early years, it seemed at times as if we were a collection of strangers trying to execute ministry. For the last three years, we've been playing catch-up with the infrastructure of the church, which means getting people plugged into small groups where they can mature and thrive.

But through our growing pains, God has been faithful, and he's allowed us to grow. Our attendance has grown twenty-five percent a year almost from the beginning and we're now at about 1,500 people a weekend.

Looking ahead, I see four major challenges for us at Calvary Church Newport Mesa:

1. How do we meet the challenge to stay fresh? Because the alternative is stagnation and death, we have to fight against the "same old, same old."
2. How do we reconcile the tension of buildings and budgets? The institutional components of "church" are very real, and they're much more difficult with an age group that has very limited resources. How do we grow

larger as a church but grow smaller (i.e., more community) at the same time? This generation is skeptical of anything "big."

3. How do we think through and respond to the cultural diversity at our doorstep? How do we serve as a unifying force for the physical community in which we live?

4. How do we give away ministry? How do we successfully adapt the model we've developed at Calvary to other communities?

These are our challenges as we enter the next stage of Buster ministry. We hope our experiences and insights will help you as you begin to consider what you can do to begin reaching out to the next generation.

# Notes

## Chapter 1
## Who Are the Busters?

1. Neil Howe and Bill Strauss, *13th Gen* (New York: Vintage Books, 1993), 33.

2. Karen Ritchie, *Marketing to Generation X* (New York: Lexington Books, 1995), 58.

3. Howe and Strauss, 145.

4. Donna Gaines, *Teenage Wasteland* (New York: Pantheon Books, 1991), 253.

## Chapter 2
## Of Boomers and Busters

1. Ritchie, 21.

2. Lawrence J. Bradford and Claire Raines, *Twentysomething* (New York: MasterMedia Books, 1992), 5.

## Chapter 4
## Anything Goes

1. Robert S. Ellwood, *The Sixties' Spiritual Awakening* (New Brunswick, N.J.: Rutgers University Press, 1994), 13.

2. Ellwood, 12.

## Chapter 5
## Nobody's Home

1. Howe and Strauss, 65.

2. Ritchie, 41.

3. Howe and Strauss, 65.

4. Ritchie, 39.

5. Leighton Ford, *The Power of Story* (Colorado Springs: NavPress, 1994), 63.

## Chapter 6
## The Electronic Playroom

1. Neil Postman, *Amusing Ourselves to Death* (New York: Viking Penguin, 1985), 142.

2. George Barna, *Baby Busters: The Disillusioned Generation* (Chicago: Northfield Publishing, 1994), 80.

3. Ritchie, 116–17.

4. Postman, 87.

5. Steven Gibb, *Twentysomething, Floundering, and Off the Yuppie Track* (Chicago: Noble Press, 1992), 16.

## Chapter 7
## Redefining the American Dream

1. Jeff Giles, "Generalizations X," *Newsweek* (June 6, 1994), 62.

2. Frederick R. Strobel, *Upward Dreams, Downward Mobility* (Lanham, 'Md.: Rowman and Littlefield, 1993), 159.

## Chapter 8
## Let's Get Spiritual

1. Sarah Ferguson, "The Comfort of Being Sad," *Utne Reader*, 62.

2. Douglas Coupland, *Life After God* (New York: St. Martin's Press, 1995), 273.

3. Ferguson, 62.

4. Gaines, 243.

5. Ford, 171.

## Chapter 9
## Walls and Bridges: How Busters View the Church

1. Coupland, 359.

## Chapter 10
## The Four R's: A Buster Primer

1. Coupland, 182–83.

2. Ibid.

# Chapter 14
## Lead Me On: Leading Busters and
## Developing Buster Leaders

1. Bradford and Raines, 124.
2. Bradford and Raines, 125–26.
3. Ibid.
4. Ibid.
5. Ibid.

## WILLOW CREEK
RESOURCES

*This resource was created to serve you.*

It is just one of many ministry tools that are part of the Willow Creek Resources® line, published by the Willow Creek Association together with Zondervan Publishing House. The Willow Creek Association was created in 1992 to serve a rapidly growing number of churches from all across the denominational spectrum that are committed to helping unchurched people become fully devoted followers of Christ. There are now more than 2,500 WCA member churches worldwide.

The Willow Creek Association links like-minded leaders with each other and with strategic vision, information, and resources in order to build prevailing churches. Here are some of the ways it does that:

- **Church Leadership Conferences**—3 1/2 -day events, held at Willow Creek Community Church in South Barrington, IL, that are being used by God to help church leaders find new and innovative ways to build prevailing churches that reach unchurched people.

- **The Leadership Summit**—a once-a-year event designed to increase the leadership effectiveness of pastors, ministry staff, volunteer church leaders, and Christians in business.

- **Willow Creek Resources®**—to provide churches with a trusted channel of ministry resources in areas of leadership, evangelism, spiritual gifts, small groups, drama, contemporary music, and more. For more information, call Willow Creek Resources® at 800/876-7335. Outside the US call 610/532-1249.

- **WCA News**—a bimonthly newsletter to inform you of the latest trends, resources, and information on WCA events from around the world.

- **The Exchange**—our classified ads publication to assist churches in recruiting key staff for ministry positions.

- **The Church Associates Directory**—to keep you in touch with other WCA member churches around the world.

- **WillowNet**—an Internet service that provides access to hundreds of Willow Creek messages, drama scripts, songs, videos and multimedia suggestions. The system allows users to sort through these elements and download them for a fee.

- **Defining Moments**—a monthly audio journal for church leaders, in which Lee Strobel asks Bill Hybels and other Christian leaders probing questions to help you discover biblical principles and transferable strategies to help maximize your church's potential.

For conference and membership information please write or call:

Willow Creek Association
P.O. Box 3188
Barrington, IL 60011-3188
ph: (847) 765-0070
fax: (847) 765-5046
www.willowcreek.org

Printed in the United States
1262200005B/46